Wake Dry Bones

An Autobiography of Truth and Trust

B. STANLEY TIESZEN

WESTBOW
PRESS®
A DIVISION OF THOMAS NELSON
& ZONDERVAN

This book is a work of non-fiction. Unless otherwise noted, the author and the publisher make no explicit guarantees as to the accuracy of the information contained in this book and in some cases, names of people and places have been altered to protect their privacy.

WestBow Press books may be ordered through booksellers or by contacting:

WestBow Press
A Division of Thomas Nelson & Zondervan
1663 Liberty Drive
Bloomington, IN 47403
www.westbowpress.com
844-714-3454

Because of the dynamic nature of the Internet, any web addresses or links contained in this book may have changed since publication and may no longer be valid. The views expressed in this work are solely those of the author and do not necessarily reflect the views of the publisher, and the publisher hereby disclaims any responsibility for them.

Any people depicted in stock imagery provided by Getty Images are models, and such images are being used for illustrative purposes only. Certain stock imagery © Getty Images.

Scripture quotations marked (NIV) are taken from the Holy Bible, New International Version®, NIV®. Copyright © 1973, 1978, 1984, 2011 by Biblica, Inc.® Used by permission of Zondervan. All rights reserved worldwide. www.zondervan.com The "NIV" and "New International Version" are trademarks registered in the United States Patent and Trademark Office by Biblica, Inc.®

Scripture marked (KJV) taken from the King James Version of the Bible.

ISBN: 978-1-6642-8626-9 (sc)
ISBN: 978-1-6642-8628-3 (hc)
ISBN: 978-1-6642-8627-6 (e)

Library of Congress Control Number: 2023910286

Print information available on the last page.

WestBow Press rev. date: 06/09/2023

CONTENTS

INTRODUCTION

The news of a young woman's health issue was announced after a Bible study I attended recently, and the purpose, of course, was to bring her before the Lord in prayer. It was announced as well that we needed to hurry, as the proposed one-hour Bible study / prayer meeting had only five minutes of time remaining. We were asked if there were other people who should be remembered, and the ones mentioned were the pastor and three deacons who were on their way to a denominational conference. Our host, also the mother of the woman with the health issue, volunteered to pray, and within several short minutes, we were dismissed. As I drove home, my heart was sad, and without explaining any of this to my wife, I retired for the night.

While lying there in my bed, I asked God what he thought about our meeting, and I wasn't surprised at all when I awoke then, late in the night. I was reminded of the many times my wife and I had gone to prayer before we retired. We love this time together. It seems to represent a roundup of sorts, a time when we share the things of the day, and generally they represent our work and close family. Then we pray. There isn't anything here that should make one sad, but I had never before seen it in the light of that Bible study. It was deficient.

Over the following days, I rehearsed this meeting time and the summation of that event. What did it lack? If I had been the leader, what would I have done differently? No one at the meeting deliberately acted with indifference toward the church. In fact, I am sure they felt as though great things had happened. Or had they? My thoughts immediately went to a conversation I had with a friend a number of years earlier. He and his wife, like us, shared the closing time of the day in prayer together. Then one evening, she surprised him with the question "Why aren't there any tears when you pray?" And as you might guess, everything became silent. I am not convinced that she believed they should weep together each evening in order to appeal to heaven for the needs of life. I do sense though that she was wondering about the lack of passion, about the heartfelt need to truly invite heaven into their circumstances and the circumstances of others, to pray so sufficiently as to reorder the events of someone's existence in order that God would have preeminence. And this raises a deeper question; could this be a characteristic that typifies a true warrior, someone with boldness and purpose, someone who would be scared of nothing except the fear of standing before God one day, having owned the tools of battle and yet having never employed them? This does sound confrontational; however, when we pray for something or even someone, are we not actually praying against something else? I am convinced that many in the church would confess they really have no idea what it might look like to be a warrior. Their hearts tell them that they desire to stand up for the right, and they want to represent Christ in both the activities of church and in community, but they are unsure what to do. While the very nature, the true identity one might say, of a warrior is to represent the affairs of his or her kingdom, we have somehow been led to understand that the totality of this occurs within the church and during one hour of time. Although some churches have midweek services, this could come to mean busyness for the family and an overly extended church commitment. Consequently, this, for many, has been abandoned.

What few understand is that many of the things that are proposed as sound investments in church or community come to war against the true advancements of the kingdom. As Christ followers, however, we must come to believe that the forward movement of kingdom affairs is paramount. So what is that really about? What must I do to promote these affairs, and what do I need to become? I don't think for a minute that the church suffers a general reluctance for this activity. On the contrary, I believe the church has many who look to be challenged in this way. So we look to the scriptures to follow the lead of great individuals, but those like John the Baptist can be intimidating. It was said of him, "Among those born of women there has not risen anyone greater than John the Baptist" (Matthew 11:11b NIV). This same passage goes on to say, "Yet he who is least in the kingdom of heaven is greater than he. From the days of John the

Baptist until now, the kingdom of heaven has been forcefully advancing, and forceful men lay hold of it."

To be this kind of Christian is not an easy task. To begin with, we ask ourselves, do I have to look and dress like John the Baptist? We all know that's not what's expected, and yet what is the key? Clearly the scripture here is stirring our curiosity to where we must pick up that baton, and to begin, we are obliged to honestly confess before God that this is what we truly desire. So first and foremost, it becomes a commitment to a task while coming clean with the fact, secondly, that we cannot do this on our own. These then come to define a multifaceted adventure—one, however, that can be achieved. No, it's never completed, because the training becomes an intense battleground in itself, but as we follow the persuasion of our tender and thirsty hearts, it can be done. As Christians, we will want to be warriors.

Without criticizing what others did that night at the prayer meeting, I decided to amp up things for us a bit. Prayer, after all, should be the backbone of what God intends to do in both the church and the home. If we are weak in this, we are likely weak in other areas as well. You may want to quit when pressure is brought to bear, but you will instead choose to become resolute (constantly pursuing a purpose). From here, God may take you into a territory or an economy that is unique to your existence, but you will learn about true faith as you have never known before. You are standing at the threshold of opportunity, not only the opportunity of a lifetime but opportunity that will stretch into eternity.

In a vision, the Old Testament prophet Ezekiel was taken to the middle of a valley. It is there on the valley floor that he is led back and forth among many dry bones. And then the Lord has an unusual conversation with him. He asks Ezekiel if these bones can live, and it's as though Ezekiel is in desperation before the Lord when he answers him, "Oh Sovereign Lord, you alone know." Then God said to Ezekiel,

> "Prophesy to these bones and say to them, 'Dry bones, hear the word of the Lord! This is what the Sovereign Lord says to these bones: I will make breath enter you, and you will come to life. I will attach tendons to you and make flesh come upon you and cover you with skin; I will

put breath in you, and you will come to life. Then you will know that I am the Lord.' So I prophesied as I was commanded. And as I was prophesying there was a noise, a rattling sound, and the bones came together, bone to bone. I looked, and tendons and flesh appeared on them and skin covered them, but there was no breath in them. Then he said to me, Prophesy to the breath; prophesy son of man, and say to it, 'This is what the Sovereign Lord says: Come from the four winds O breath and breathe into these slain, that they may live.' So I prophesied as he commanded me, and breathe entered them; they came to life and stood up on their feet-a vast army." (Ezekiel 37:4–10 NIV)

This prophecy was for the nation of Israel, and although it cannot be twisted to mean anything for the church today, it should stir our hearts. We can quickly come to the understanding that it was God alone who could breathe life into something that has no life. In our climate of too much money, too much high culture, too much of everything except faith, hope, and love, we could easily say that ours has become a dry and thirsty land. Apathy has become the norm; complacency and even indolence define the ambition among even Christians in our society. The question of prayer then could be easily asked of us, where are the tears?

But it's not too late; there is much to be done, and God longs to challenge us with the real work of the kingdom. As he brings the eternities of past and future to a meeting place, time and destiny await us. What will be our defining purpose? What is it that tugs at our hearts, that objective that seems so distant and yet haunts us to no end? How can God use us in the church and community that will contribute to bringing heaven and earth to that point of contact? We were not born into the family of God to simply one day ship off to heaven, as some believe, and leave this rotten old world behind. We were reborn to follow the example of Christ, to make a difference.

In the pages that follow, we want to explore the true meaning of that discipleship and to better understand why the Bible so frequently uses strong military terms for its discussion of Christian life. We will discover how peace-loving people can engage in combat and how combative people can be peace-loving. We will be challenged to look over our shoulder, so to speak, and to ask ourselves some rather serious questions as we reflect on our godly progress. Some may come to realize that they have reached a plateau, that their testimony is old and stale. Even some pastors use messages from the archives, showing evidence of burnout or even flatlining. Nonetheless, life does go on, and if perchance the pilgrimage of our soul, somehow having been weakened by the anxieties of this world, needs a reevaluation, honest confession can take us there.

Over the past several years, I had the privilege of helping a woman with some menial chores around her home. This lady has been a Christ follower for many years and had recently lost her husband to cancer. While I worked, we chatted together, and some of her past seemed to surface. I rather casually made the suggestion that she take a more serious look at these personal offenses of years gone by. Her response was quick and direct. "Why would I want to go back to that?" My answer was simple, "The truth will set you free." Who among us doesn't have some baggage that has been tucked away somewhere in the closet of our mind? No one knows except we ourselves, and with the schedules and responsibilities that are handed out, there just isn't enough time to deal with these issues. And yet we are crippled because of them, failing to learn and experience scriptural passages and principles in which God himself wants to liberate us. We will awake the kingdom spirit within us when we, as Christ's disciples, follow a different kingdom philosophy and find personal healing for our very soul. The spiritual energy that comes from these experiences is not only life transforming for us; it influences those around us, thereby becoming the forceful advancement of kingdom affairs talked about by Matthew and lived out by John the Baptizer. As well, this energy could not be humanly engineered or manipulated; we could only give ourselves to something bigger than our own self-centeredness.

In Ezekiel's time, a vast army was assembled as the result of one man's willingness to listen to God and then, in obedience, to act. It's true that this was a vision; however, consistently throughout scripture, our God and the God of the Israelites showed himself capable of this type of supernatural display. And so today we are each invited as well to experience a new Pentecostal power, to be part of an energy force that lives and works above and beyond all of the demonic forces that plague our places of work and play. One cannot read the Gospels and on into the book of Acts without longing to be added to those who faithfully embarked on a commission that eventually spread across the globe. These were truly the warriors of their time, and they call to us. However, any lasting activity will be sparked only by the intention of our own will, a consent of the heart, thereby becoming a volitional response to the Spirit that lives within. Throughout life, this is all optional, as the scriptures will tell us, "If a man remains in me and I in him he will bear much fruit. Apart from me you can do nothing" (Luke 15:5 NIV). Finally, when we have been sufficiently challenged, who among us would dare to enter heaven's gates with only a scratch to prove our identity as a disciple of Jesus Christ? Others, as we shall discover, paid so dearly.

1

THE CHURCH

Whatever happens, conduct yourselves in a manner worthy of
the gospel of Christ. Then. ... I will know that you stand firm in
one spirit, contending as one man for the faith of the gospel.
—Philippians 1:27 (NIV)

Hanging on the wall of our home library is a picture of an old Native
American man. Actually, this picture is a black-and-white photograph
taken in the year 1926 and is nearly life-size. I found it in an antique store,
hanging way up high on a wall, as if to be out of reach of a would-be buyer.
Instantly, I knew that I had to have it because he represented so perfectly
the real first people of the North American plains. The man's face, half-
bowed as if in quiet contemplation, shows deep wrinkles typical of a life
spent on the open prairie, one moment traveling under the hot summer sun
and the next hunting on horseback in the blinding snow or freezing rain.
Quite frequently, I will lounge in this room, read, or, more often, quietly
sit and contemplate life on my own, and then he will be there, his head
turned downward, his eyes open only slightly. After careful observation,
it becomes obvious that what he remembers of life is very different and
far more distant than anything most of us could ever imagine. His name
was Black Belly, and he must have been in his late teens or early twenties
when General George Armstrong Custer's Battle of the Little Bighorn was
fought. And there is little or no question as to whether he played a part in
this bloody massacre, as Black Belly was a Cheyenne warrior.

Aside from the battles where Black Belly and his people fought other Native tribes as well as the White settlers, he could recall the many times when he and his so-called red brothers searched to find the roaming buffalo. If he could speak, he might tell you of chasing them down and killing a select few to provide food, shelter, and clothing for his family. He could recollect the many times their village moved and the process that was involved in this picturesque and unforgettable lifestyle. And likewise, he will remember how drastically and dramatically life on the open prairie changed with the so-called settling of the west, the encroachment of European Whites. Even now, you can see from the picture that his shoulders are covered with a woolen blanket typical of a government supply; the hunting is gone forever, and the tepee has been replaced with a log hut. Freedom has become confined to a reservation, and the challenges of everyday life will rest on the shoulders of the big chief in Washington. This is what I see in the tired and worn face of the early American warrior Black Belly.

To the cowboy, which I'm privileged to have once called myself, the Native way of life had a nostalgia as well as an equal share in the frontier lifestyle I once tried to emulate, all the while realizing that the Native tribes were primitive, uncivilized if you will. The Indians of the plains were savage, a very disputed accusation, which, although this can be proven from historical literature, I prefer to view differently. I am cognizant of the fact that there are those who might resent any comparison or parallel between our ethnicities. And I understand all too plainly that these were warring people given to much superstition. They exhibited a pluralistic religiosity, believing in a God and yet worshipping the sun. It was not uncommon to torture themselves while seeking the favor of Old Man Coyote, and some still practice the sun dance, which has proven to be extremely destructive for their people. As I frequently use them in illustrations, I am aware of these vast differences between them and the so-called Christian warrior. As well, I remind myself continually of the night-and-day differences in our objectives. We may talk about them today and attempt to compare the activity of a Christian man with a Native warrior, but it's only an attempt at an isolated characteristic. We today have a sheltered and restricted existence. Using this culture as a method of exciting Christians to become something they can never duplicate is in some ways unfair; however, there are certain characteristics that we just cannot deny as being applicable to the life of a true Christian. We will want to look at these as well as other key identity characteristics of a Christian warrior and discover if there even is such a thing. Indulge me if you will, as in much of this document, I have borrowed from this somewhat forgotten lifestyle. And finally, in our modern-day society, civilized and sophisticated as we are, be careful not to get heady. Through humility and truth come understanding, from understanding comes healing, and from healing comes an awakening, thereby augmenting the strength of the church—the subject of this book.

It has been with these and similar thoughts deeply embedded in my mind that I have lived, studied, and gathered a lifetime of illustrations. And coupled with time, they seem to have created a long list of friends, writing companions if you will, who together have augmented my pilgrimage toward personal spiritual growth. Not one of us, Black Belly, myself, or anyone, were naturally born warriors; we are groomed to become them. As I write, it is again from my life and experience both in and outside of the church. You will notice the ongoing need for transparency and willingness, personally, to embrace change. Most often, this is the result of a spiritual nudge or a subtle suggestion from others that we become more aware of a character flaw or an attitude adjustment. From a nonverbal position, we may feel at times somewhat coerced to where we either resist or continue to move closer toward the center of our relationship with Jesus Christ. Biblical Christianity, however, is intentional, and warriors are proven stuff. Regardless of the pain and often the embarrassment or regret from the past, they will move forward at all costs.

Over many years of Christian life and activity, there have been few questions that have stirred my mind and curiously provoked more attention than the following: Where are the real warriors of the church? What do they look like, and what activities are they engaged in that seem to rise above others? Are some hiding out for fear of intimidation, or do they lack proper instruction? Worse still, has the church, in all its busyness, recognized these sufficiently to give an anointed platform, thereby augmenting the course of ministry?

The response to my own question, after taking some serious time to evaluate it, was that I not only needed to explore the topic further, but I needed to face it.

It's much like so many things that develop in the life of a Christian, where we change, and the church and the world around us change alongside. It's not for reasons of carnality or rebelliousness that things change; it is because our past is reflected through this ever-changing set of circumstances, like the sun as it moves about a room, casting a moving shadow. So, too, we continue to see things in the changing light of our experience, and I am challenged by this type of examination. I have purposely kept my study books and Bible just beyond reach, as I sense the need to write my first and last impressions; this is not as much a theological discourse as it is a recollection of my experience. After all, our lives within the local church are constantly under that specific scrutiny, and they are shaped accordingly. As a result, giving ourselves to be like Christ within the context of a specific church emulates—or suffers, one could say—the character traits of that particular organization, some traits being good and some not so much. Honest confession would admit that denominations as well as church organizations do have a mindset; what they teach is not always followed by what is lived out, and the demand to conform often overrides good instruction.

What continually comes to mind is my own worldview. What do I believe, and to what institution of learning do I give myself that allows the continual reshaping of my mind toward the church, the body of believers? Needless to say, there are those who go along with the tide, never realizing the total responsibility of their belief system, how to build it up, or possibly how they might defend it one day. My particular vocation, for example, depends heavily on architectural correctness; however, society has taught us that the decisions of design, textures, and colors are often made by popular opinion. So as these occasions arise, I don't apologize in saying, "Well, there you go; here is living proof that even without knowledge, one can have an opinion." There is a penalty for this behavior, both in the field of architecture and in the church. Consequently, there has been and will continue to be an evolutionary process within the church, one that will prove authenticity or one that will be counterfeit. Evolution in itself suggests movement, progress, and development; however, the church must continually face its north.

So what is the true church? In my early experience, it became a community of like-minded and some not so like-minded Christ followers. It was in the church that I found acceptance. Through compassion and instruction, I learned of forgiveness, and upon confession, I found salvation. It was in the church, and among those who belonged to that great body, that the God of the universe showed me his love and I was drawn to him. From this fragile point, I experienced deliverance from satanic influence. In the church, I was introduced to new friends, a new vocabulary, and a totally new lifestyle; and through my new relationship with Jesus Christ, I found peace. I began to learn about real joy and happiness. With faithful church attendance, I could get up every morning without regret or another headache; and in the church, I began the lifelong process of healing for my very soul. I must say that I love the church, and as difficult as it is to reflect on it from this perspective of elapsed time, it has been within the church, within relationships of both harmony and discord, that I experienced all of real family life.

Life in church isn't always wonderful. Very early on, we discover that the church is full of people, all with problems just like us, and what's more is that they are in the process of healing as well. This body of believing people has an organized political structure; it has a set of rules and guidelines that are not a handout. There is a power pole, and the person at the top may not be the pastor or the priest. Also, there is a way you do things and a way you get things done. It's continually said here that God looks at the heart, but believe me, the right set of clothes could get you an assignment very quickly. This is being pretty critical when these rules are little different than any business or organization where you get out of it just what you put in. However, the initial luster wares off quickly, leaving us to jockey for position, and just like any classroom, we must learn to work together, and this can take time.

God's design on church didn't leave us without instruction, however; nor did he abandon us to do things alone. The scriptures give us a template of sorts, and the ever-abiding presence of the Holy Spirit divinely enables us to do his bidding. Beyond that, God has endowed each follower with spiritual gifts or charisms designed and intended to build up the body of Christ. Personally, I am totally amazed how God has equipped the church. There was never a mistake with this intricate design, and Paul, speaking to the church at Corinth, said, "You do not lack any spiritual gift as you eagerly wait for our Lord Jesus Christ to be revealed" (1 Corinthians 1:7b NIV). As wonderful as all of this is for the individual and the church, for me it hasn't come without a price. To learn of the endowment of spiritual giftedness and to understand its working will forever be a mystery held in the storehouse of heaven. You simply cannot package this all up; nor is there a promise that the church will recognize it. My experience has taught me that the use of these gifts, or should I say how the gifts are intended to be employed, and the creativity of their design are wrapped up in a vocabulary all their own; humility, availability, obedience, and surprise are all couched in the same setting as listening, sensitivity, waiting, and watching. God will use our gifts and us in a place of his choosing, and at the time of his choosing. The entire performance of any gifted activity God has ordained will come through prayer and proceed in prayer. Rest assured, you will be certain in the end that we were only an instrument, and God did the work.

Some of my greatest disappointments have been in the church. God has always used these times, however, as a launching pad for further instruction. Life is difficult, and the scriptures warn us of this. God's intention, however, is to build character in us, and this never comes without pain. I want to say that in my experience, it never gets easier. Even when we pray in earnest regarding our difficulties, we learn that Jesus does not fit our expectations; he reorients us to fit his image. The consolation, of course, is that we are reminded of God's promise to carry on his good work in us to completion until the day of Jesus Christ (Philippians 1:6 NIV).

So again, to explore the topic of church is not too complicated; to face it is quite another story. It has demanded a transparency of heart and an ongoing confession. While I am committed to this personal inquiry, the pages that follow were emotional for me to write. Although the past feelings of anger were not lost in the futility of bitterness and resentment, at times I could bury my head in my hands. As I wrote, often even pointing a finger, my ambition was only that the church, more so each individual believer, would find his or her place of fruitful service within it and more so within the community that we have been placed. So in this book, we shall start, if only in some small way, adventuring into the real world of our own lives as disciples in the church of Jesus Christ. We will look closely through my personal experience and attempt to see whether any threads of principle emerge, ones that have been employed or denied, thereby altering the course of our lives and consequently the strength of the greater church.

2

OUTSIDE THE CAMP

For the kingdom of God is not a matter of talk but of power.
—1 Corinthians 4: 20 (NIV)

Having come from a background of goal-oriented, semi-achievers, I viewed my family with a reasonable amount of respect. So as a young man looking toward the future, I could see that living somewhat within that context could have some possibilities. Many of the activities that my family engaged in became my interests as well, so it wasn't too difficult to give a listening ear even in my restless, formative, teenage years. I can well remember a few things that were said over those unforgettable times that seemed not only to resonate within my person; they set up permanent residence in my soul. Often I would weigh out these impressions during a particular time of crisis, trying desperately to see how they would stack up, so to speak. One of these thoughts was in the form of two scripture verses found in Revelation 3: 15–16 (NIV), "I know your deeds, that you are neither cold nor hot. I wish you were either one or the other! So, because you are lukewarm, neither hot nor cold—I am about to spit you out of my mouth." These verses were terrifying to me, and each one had a significant impact on my life. Today, I view them from a larger perspective, probably not quite as personal as had been initially intended; however, this passage has in mind a spiritual examination. Written to the early churches by John the apostle, I am sure that it has put many on edge, just as it did for me. It asks a question: what are you doing in your Christian existence that has any lasting value?

Without question, this passage became part of the driving force that led me to the point of my conversion. The idea of God Almighty one day literally turning his back toward me had impact. After that turning point in my life, I committed myself to what I knew then about Christianity. And having come from a legalistic background, this is where I began to direct the character adjustments of my life. Although I had no idea what would be asked of me, my heart told me that I wanted desperately to identify with the new focus of my life, and this step of obedience itself was a volitional act that testified to the work of Christ's regeneration in my life. Looking back now, this seemed to initiate as well as confirm the fresh direction of my newfound faith, and I followed it immediately by obedience in baptism, confirming this commitment.

It was with this mindset that I came to the conclusion that Christians shouldn't smoke cigarettes. So with my best foot forward, I determined that I would quit (good luck with that)! Each night, I would go out to a particular place and hold a little service of sorts, where I would throw my smokes out the window and make a rather stern vow to stop this filthy habit. I am certain that heaven got a charge out of it, especially when I would get a brand-new pack first thing the next morning. This went on for some time until one day I sensed a little voice inside me saying, "Bill, I think it would be great for you to quit smoking cigarettes, but quite honestly, there are some other things that lack attention." And that's when we stopped playing church and got on with a personal relationship. If you were to know me today, you might easily find something to criticize, but you have no idea the brokenness that earlier defined me as a person. Occasionally now, God will show me something in a new light, and I will again know there is a change in the making.

The story about my cigarette habit, although you got the short version, (and I did eventually quit) drew a line in the sand of my Christian walk that took me literally years to discern. Subconsciously, I had not only connected my relationship with Christ to the local church, but I enrolled in their mindset as well. Unknowingly, I had conformed to a process, a mentality unofficially known as *bounded set*, which we will discuss later. While I desperately needed and loved church life, little did I know that it had no control over my type of growth or the rate at which I would develop. Equally as meaningful, I saw that the church could not contain or identify the outward expression of my faith or my giftedness. As opportunities to serve Christ came my way, I would try to connect them directly with the church, like there needed to be some automatic attachment. The church saw this happening, and while never assisting in any way, they eventually became the beneficiary; those I affected began to attend my church. This began to stir a curiosity satisfied only by the continual study of scriptures and life itself. While being respected in my church as a man hard after God, the responsibilities that the church handed out, some of which came by popular vote, seldom proved to be completely successful. This plagued me. Somehow, I thought, I was not conforming; I was an independent, so to speak. These job descriptions failed to bring me satisfaction, only profile. I sensed as well that I had gained little favor; maybe I was even viewed as rebellious or just not a team player. I didn't know. While none of this ever proved to be harmful, I was soon to be marked; like the kid on the playground who would not be picked for the team, he would never be acknowledged as one to help the team on to success.

My life and ministry within the church seemed to follow a pattern; opportunities would develop that were consistent with my gifting and the call that I and others saw upon my life, followed by preparation and hard work, service that would meet minimum expectation and then rejection. This became a vicious cycle with little gratification. And then I began to experience unique opportunities becoming available that hadn't originated within the church. With these opportunities, I was challenged. I found complete fulfillment, and eventually they became fruit bearing as well. While I have continually maintained my membership in our local church and supported its ministries, it has been through this pain of rejection that I have come to recognize service and dedication from another perspective.

Over the course of time, I observed a reward from this interaction with outsiders that caught me by surprise. While I say this with absolute humility, I say it with total confidence; maturity had developed, and the root system of my faith, if you will, had grown deeper. This may have occurred, possibly, through the study and preparation I had engaged in for these various ministry outlets. I do not know. (Look at Philemon 1:6 NIV). However, I experienced that this resulted in an increasing outside ministry. While church leadership recognized this effectiveness in specific areas, it was not a part of their intended ministry focus. These thoughts always provoke such curiosity, fun to talk about but not so fun to live. Honest confession, however, will tell you that the rejection part, which is often referred to as isolation, is the most difficult. It's a punishment of sorts for not being totally aligned with the organization of the church. This isn't a rebellious attitude that goes against her work; the church simply does not know what to do with certain people. In contrast, I see the church as the institution in need. The church needs a thousand other men and women just like I have described—followers who are active, creative, well read, engaged in all of life, and experiencing a vibrancy that God alone can give. These people aren't all healed up; they are just like you and I, a people in process. It is these, men and women alike, however, who give themselves to that process, and God wants to use them. Just as someone has said, "In the real world it's the wounded that heal" (N.T. Wright, *For All God's Worth*, p. 21).

For too long, I had held a particular Bible verse at arm's length, wondering if I would ever pass the grade and be used for the purpose of calling others to obedience. This sounds awfully pastoral, I have thought, and yet, seemingly without reserve, God would use me for these purposes among others. As a result, I have come to believe that it has only been guilt, not lack of Christlikeness, that intimidates us, prohibiting godly performance. The verse I am referring to concludes a rather small but powerful passage found in 2 Corinthians 10:6 (NIV), "And we will be ready to punish every act of disobedience, once your obedience is complete." I am not intending to disappoint anyone, but my obedience is in a continual state of repair. It's not that I live in deliberate sin; I just need constant attention, and an honest confession here would include the church at large. What the verse is saying is that you cannot teach forgiveness if you cannot forgive. Get a hold of this; it's only as we walk in the light, which is walking in obedience to what the Spirit is saying moment by moment, that we gain credibility in our circle of influence. This favor then should begin within the church community and extend into the street, and it's here in these two places where we have great impact. My long experience agrees with the stern language of authors Hauerwas and Willimon: "All Christians, by their baptism, are 'ordained' to share in Christ's work in the world. There is no healing, counseling, witnessing, speaking, interpretation, living, or dying the clergy can do that is not the responsibility of every other Christian" (*Resident Aliens*, p. 113).

In a book that I was recently given, the writer introduced me to somewhat of a new vocabulary that I believe applies here. The author began by introducing four relatively uncommon words into the chapter. As he did, my curiosity was stirred, and it wasn't until after focusing on one key sentence that I got the picture. It reads like this: "The gospel is an alchemy of grace, which transforms by application, as a medicine is applied to a wound by a physician" (Alister McGrath, *The Passionate Intellect*, p. 50). One of the four words that I spoke of and used here is *alchemy*, which means "the infant stage of chemistry, as astrology was of astronomy—its chief aims being to transmute the other metals into gold and to discover the elixir of life." The word study for me was *alchemy, transmutation, elixir*, and *tincture*. This was healing for me and continues to be so.

It's in this setting that the Alchemist, God by his Spirit, is doing his finest work in our lives and the chemistry is taking place; however, there is conflict. This is where composition meets competition. Our lives, on the one hand, are where God wants this transforming energy to play music to those around us, thus the transmutation, making the foreign metals around us to be like gold and prolonging life. In this process, one gives themselves as a student to learn as well as be taught (and there is a difference), resulting in a tint, divinely added by the Instructor himself, the tincture. This, again, is the composition, the overflow of a life, the music that the individual Christian plays to his or her church community and the world in audience.

Organized church, on the other hand, could easily become the competition, as it's in constant pursuit of those who fit within a particular mold, ones who meet their particular criterion. It's here where the gifted Christ follower, like myself, could be held captive, and it's here where the very hypocrisy of the scribes and Pharisees, scorned by the church, could again be the church. It is lived out in the attempts of a controlled organization to somehow replicate the biological church. Throughout my life in this institution, I seem to have failed, but I failed only in the idea of not fitting its agenda. This organized church has fabricated a template; they've "trimmed the picture of our personalities to fit they're mass-produced frames" (Os Guinness, *The Call*, p. 21). "The truth is not that God is finding us a place for our gifts but that God has created us and our gifts for a place of his choosing-and we will be ourselves when we are finally there" (Os Guinness, *The Call,* p. 47). The idea of coming alongside for the sake of harmony and purpose for me represented years of smothering fruitlessness, being neutered if you will. And this was said to be the result, somehow, of not fitting the pastoral vision. I would say that this lacks insight and has stifled the greater work of the church.

I am not advocating at all that individuals leave the church to start their own private nest of like-minded protesters. What I am saying is that the outreach potential of the church, the warriors if you will, is far more extensive than has ever been imagined; I am saying that those who do not actually compliment the church and its agenda should find another commissioning. And yet they sit idle, not knowing how to engage. They have become abandoned. The church will be enlarged when at last the individual Christ follower finds freedom and instruction to minister. This is the job of pastor, to equip God's people for acts of service and to spin them off for their duty.

As I have operated a business for most of my adult life, I found that my best investment into the lives of my employees was to find the key to their motivation, then give them the necessary tools and a job that needed their specific skill set. Of course this had to fit within the product ability of our company, but that was always our primary objective. Although I stood prepared to give further instruction as the leader and administrator, it became theirs to stand up to the challenge. I never had the right to smother them or control their future, only compliment it. I recall one very specific occasion when I had been working in the shop area and that small voice said very plainly, "You are done here; you need to leave this area of work, or you will stifle the real potential of your shop foreman." Fortunately for me, I listened and was free to share my thoughts with this man. He no longer needed the all-seeing eye of the boss hovering over him. While maintaining the guidelines of our business, he was free to explore complementary methods of product appearance, assembly, and finish. Consequently, he continues to find his true potential, and obviously we were the better for it. Contrary to the way business is generally run, I needed to learn that I never owned these men; they were given to me to further develop what God had placed in their hearts to do. Again, while maintaining the guidelines of our business, this did alter seriously our finished product and raised the level of quality dramatically.

In fairness, I must also say that there are those who fit the church perfectly as they serve her need for organizational structure. I applaud those who carry on these various tasks. The failure has come, however, when the job description of everyone else becomes laity; no worthy title, no commissioning, no anointing, no training, no platform, no assignment, no accountability, no prayerful support, and no sense of worth. These are the ones in the trenches, the grunts; they're lives are on trial every moment of every day. The church has never initiated these with a purposeful assignment; those who serve outside do so because they have been dismissed. They failed to pass the bar. There will be no gratitude shown for being misplaced, and at life's end, there will be no diamond-studded tie clasp. We have come to aggrandize the platform of the walled church to where it has become the absolute pinnacle of power and prestige, leaving others who are gifted and ambitious to either conform to strict qualifications and a time-consuming agenda or to be ostracized. I must admit that while this has been painful for me to experience, the outcome of the lesson is simple; my place of service is not in church leadership or platform activity. With the fear that many within the church fall under this category, it becomes obligatory that further instruction be given. Those forgotten ones must know that they are not alone, and they must understand as well that the call to and the qualifications for fulfillment and service reside within their very being, and they must pursue it.

Paul Hiebert, in his fine book *Anthropological Reflections on Missional Issues*, introduces the concept mentioned earlier, "Bounded sets and Centered sets." This is echoed by Jim Peterson in *Church without Walls*. Both of these men have discovered through study what I learned personally over years of painful experience.

> We are accustomed to defining the church within a certain rectangular enclosure. We work at clarifying who is in, who is out; what the leadership structure is to be and not to be; what we believe and do not believe; which activities belong and which do not; and what behavior is appropriate and what is not. So the line that is drawn between insiders and outsiders is clearly drawn. Hiebert calls this bounded-set thinking. That is, there is

a boundary that sets the standard. One either qualifies or is rejected; it's pass or fail. What I'm advocating … is that we move from bounded-set thinking to what Hiebert refers to as "centered-set" thinking in our church. In centered-set, what counts is how much each member is moving in relationship to the center. Belonging, in this case, is not a matter of performing according to an agreed - upon profile, it is a matter of living and acting out of commitment to a common center. The focus is on the center and on pointing people to that center. Process is more important than definitions. Centered-set thinking affirms initiatives that would otherwise not find a place. It rewards creativity.

Christ is that center!

Although some of the lessons of serving in my early life and development seemed to meet minimal expectation, somehow through the sincerity of my own heart, a clear path began to show itself. And having been blessed with the creativity mentioned here, I've discovered that I am a guy outside the camp. In many cases, the church has yet to identify those who are of this nature. They have, in fact, failed to officially recognize and commission this particular expertise as it exposes itself in a multitude of ways. These individuals are warriors, every bit as much as those who hold positions of higher leadership. They are indispensable warriors who don't hang around camp picking up the trash or hoping for a tidy little theological sparring with a fellow constituent over petty issues. This warrior is outside the camp and thinks in those terms. Sad to say, he or she is self-equipped and actually, for the most part, ill prepared. Along with no commission, they were never anointed for their duties and yet are a vital part of the whole, an intrinsic and invaluable part of the body. Of course, similar to my experience in our company's shop, there is still accountability, but these gifted individuals must be discovered, trained, encouraged, and spun off for their duties. Working within this presents a new set of dynamics; there will be a learning curve, there will be the expense of time, there will be the pain of discovery and development, but, too, there will be fruit bearing because it works! Rejection, for me, was just another form of acceptance;

it simply finds its way in another setting, no sorrow or regret but with the eyes of my heart open wide for future opportunity. Oswald Chambers says it like this: "Do you continue to go with Jesus? The way lies through Gethsemane, through the gates, outside the camp; the way is alone, and the way lies until there is no trace of footsteps left, only a voice. Follow me."

In this chapter, we exposed some private experiences of the author and their resulting conclusions. Through repetition of these events and a progressive bent toward church as an organization rather than church as a (organism?) community, we also became aware of an evolutionary downturn. In addition, the concept of a composition versus competition was introduced, giving clarity to the lack of investment on the behalf of undervalued yet gifted members.

3

THE BIG FISHERMAN

And after you have done everything to stand. Stand firm then.
—Ephesians 6:13b–14a (NIV)

It has been said that writers are the conscience of the land. We would probably agree that in today's society, this should give one a fair amount of latitude. Although it's not expected that a writer of today would share the conviction of a Christian, as much of their subject matter, at no fault of their own, would have little to do with improving or empowering the church. This author's attempts are not from the position of an authority or being the conscience of the land but as a complete transparency, a confession on his own part as being a member in particular of an organization at the point of a watershed. Quite easily, I will speak of my own experiences and how I suffered rejection and frequent times of isolation due largely to unidentified giftedness. By all probability, this is all part of the life of a Christian, or he never walked the walk. I personally came to the church from a position of dysfunction, and although this became the place where I found salvation, healing was a long way off; respectfully and somewhat regretfully, I merely conformed to another style of dysfunction.

My healing, although ongoing, has come from a combination of church life and the workaday world. When we are doing what God has intended, things just seem to go together. My findings have convinced me that it should be my "ambition to lead a quiet life, to mind my own business and to work with my hands, so that my daily life would win the respect of others and so that I wouldn't be dependent on anybody"

(1 Thessalonians 4:11–12, my own translation). This is the long and short of it, not too complicated or too difficult to live out, and it's therapeutic. The church is part of this; it's not work and then church. I carry church with me every day. It's what I live and breathe. I am the church, and the church is me. And furthermore, together with others, we are a community, one that gives itself to the fellowship of like-minded, believing (and unbelieving) people and one's that come together for the purposes defined in scripture. Acts 3:40–47 (NIV) provides a list that should be characteristic of a church gathering: repentance, baptism, teaching, fellowship, breaking bread, prayer, giving, serving, and worshiping. To put an overall label on this, it strongly suggests believing, baptizing, and belonging.

Belonging is a wonderful word. It's family. Within this context, I am cared for, encouraged, loved, instructed, and held accountable. A liturgical pastor in our community felt quite strongly that, for Christians, his church was meant to be a community where God was experienced within and among the people gathered there. His sentiment was that you can't have that experience if the church is organized like a corporation. A common reaction of visitors to the congregation that he served was that it was impossible to hide, to be anonymous there. They would sense that if they were to come back, people would get to know them, and they would have to come to terms with friendship and intimacy. This negative experience gets to the heart of what church is meant to be: a human-sized community where we are welcomed to the love of God. Wow—if it could only be that simple.

It seems that many church denominations experience greater difficulty with organizational issues in that to grow in numbers, which is touted as noble, the tendency is to adopt methods of the megachurch. This is where the church becomes secular, when we have discovered formulas for success and they are condoned because numbers represent souls. The impact this has had is huge. Some pastors have resigned the position of shepherding to be administrators, and formulas for gifted service have corralled the parishioners to be in subjection to the big kahuna, the sole visionary. *And if you fit this program, we can make you a star.* Guilt is a driving force to this madness because what Christ follower doesn't have a desire to be in support of their church? And this is tremendously important: every Christian has an inborn need to be a member in particular. When we come together with a healthy family, we want to add to that unity. From the most dynamic of personalities to the least, there is the need to belong. We must all have something to contribute; it's not a celebrity issue.

> On the contrary, those parts of the body that seem to be weaker are indispensable, and the parts that we think are less honorable we treat with special honor. And the parts that are unpresentable are treated with special modesty, while our presentable parts need no special treatment. But God has combined the members of the body and has given greater honor to the parts that lacked it, so that there should be no division in the body, but that its parts should have equal concern for each other. If one part suffers, every part suffers with it; if one part is honored, every part rejoices with it. (Ephesians 12: 22–26 NIV)

Organized church, on the other hand, is packaged for success. They even ask themselves if they are the best show in town. As a society where we are used to being entertained, it becomes easy, normal actually, to sit back and let the show begin. We are blessed when emotion wisps us off to a worship atmosphere, but emotion is shallow; it lacks connection and the strength that community can give. In the words of my English-born pastor, "It builds a faith quivering under the storms of life if things go a bit fraught" (Jacob Knee, former Episcopal and now Catholic priest). We desperately need an intimate fellowship, one where you can hear the sound of iron on iron, a sharpening of our very souls.

The business world has dramatically experienced the negative effects of a one-man visionary. Within this form of leadership, it suffers shortsightedness. In a recent study, it was learned that the investment of the entire network of employees was essential to truly find the destiny of a thriving company. A specific amount of time was given regularly for employees to brainstorm thoughts and ideas that could contribute to the company's improvement. Obviously, there were those who had less to contribute than others; however, leading, globally recognized companies continued this exercise, realizing the benefits.

Toyota is the world's most profitable car maker-by a long margin. Much of its success rests on an unmatched ability to enroll employees in the relentless pursuit of efficiency and quality. For more than 40 years Toyota's capacity for continuous improvements has been powered by a belief in the ability of "ordinary" employees to solve complex problems. While U.S. carmakers are now working hard to more fully utilize the brain power of their employees, they have paid dearly for a management system that was rooted in intellectual feudalism. (Gary Hamel, *The Future of Management*, pp. 23, 29, 57).

I find this to be mentally stimulating that big business finds a need to adopt a community atmosphere to conduct better business.

It is important to distinguish here between futile and feudal. Futile is most commonly used in a case where there is no apparent useful purpose; however, feudal suggests feudalism, which is a word defining "a system of political organization having as its basis the relation of lord to vessel" (*Webster's*). It's not too complicated, but it strongly suggests that one is subservient to another for a fee. Consequently, there is one leader, and all others are in subjection. Not only so, but all others exist only for the purpose of support. It becomes obvious that organization looks to intellectual feudalism, and organism looks to gifted laity. I could give numerous illustrations on how the church organization laid to waste ministry opportunities that had proven effective but were set aside because of the vision of the one man. The problem is that, similar to US carmakers, the congregation/community mechanism may not ever have been given time and space to express its God-given creative energy. There is a learning process here that goes beyond the weekly, formal pastoral instruction. Most have been conditioned to attend a one-hour service during which 85 percent of the congregation fails to give an ounce of energy to the next week's performance, and 15 percent are overworked. The 85 percent aren't reluctant to participate; for various reasons, they do not fit. The creativity discovered at Toyota wasn't instantaneous; it took time. They paid the price and initiated the concept. Further discovery found that the scale of contribution to improvement came from the passionate at 35 percent, the creative at 25 percent, those with initiative at 20 percent, and, actually in second to last place, the intellectual at 15 percent. While not intending to impugn those with a larger intellectual capacity, it is embarrassing; we have to believe that the majority of team players, the warriors, are sitting in the pews, either frustrated or complacent. They are nervously crossing their legs, squirming from side to side, anxiously waiting and wanting to engage. And similar to a working dog on a cattle ranch, if they aren't busy, they start to bite.

A thought that deserves consideration is that the administratively grown churches have a serious impact in the community with the so-called hands and feet ministries. Are these not sufficient to satisfy the need that some have regarding their longing to be kingdom investors? My answer comes with another question: when did it become the job of a pastor or an administration to create community jobs for its parishioners?

> We are not called to help people. We are called to follow Jesus, in whose service we learn who we are and how we are to help and be helped. Jesus, in texts like his Sermon on the Mount, robs us of our attempts to do something worthwhile for the world, something "effective" that yields results as an end in itself. His is an ethic not built upon helping people or even the results, certainly not on helping folk to be a bit better adjusted within an occupied Judea. His actions are based upon his account of how God is kind to the ungrateful and selfish, making the sun rise on the good and the bad. We are called to "be perfect" even as our Heavenly Father is. (Stanley Hauerwas and William H. Willimon, *Resident Aliens*, p. 121)

You can probably agree that as the individual disciple strives toward perfection, meaning maturity, the natural inclination is to be the hands and feet of Jesus. Furthermore, the church simply cannot reach into the individual hearts of our neighbors and friends who represent the real needs of the community. God can and will use you in unique ways that the church will never be privy to. I fear at times that the parishioner could become too busy with the jobs initiated corporately that might take them away from what really matters; some just cannot say no to busyness and the profile that busyness may gain for them.

This entire do-good idea augments yet another totally inconceivable thought, one where the pastor/administrator is the *big fisherman*. From the pulpit, the plan has been announced, "If you will bring your unsaved friends and neighbors to church, we will do our best to get them saved." It is as though the average parishioner lacks the ability to adequately articulate the Gospel message sufficiently; it's as though the clergy, through their cleverness, can somehow do what others cannot by the power of the Holy Ghost. I have said in previous documents that this may not be a sin of commission, but it surely is a sin of omission. The job of evangelism belongs to the individual Christ follower, and the job of pastor/priest is to equip this person for effective service. There is a pattern here that confirms the evolutionary downturn mentioned earlier: the pastor becomes the senior administrator and the sole visionary, followed by his tight group of pawns, all selected from the business community of successful, high-energy players. The congregation is the workforce, taught that their only significance is fitting into the big agenda. The motivation is the guilt that if you have another thought, you are not a team player; you are rebellious and hell bound. This becomes a continual safeguard for the organizational enterprise of the church. "Whenever the clergy claim some 'specialness' for their praying, witnessing, or caring, this serves to confirm the deadly, erroneous concept that the clergy are the only real ministers and that the laity exists only to support and feed these real ministers the clergy" (Hauerwas and Willimon, *Resident Aliens*, p. 113).

A second thought that could be considered here is this: were the thoughts displayed here spawned by bitterness of heart? My answer goes back to when the apostles Peter and Paul got into a disagreement over the issue of the Jews and the Gentiles (Acts 10:9–35 NIV). Through a dream, God made it perfectly clear to Peter that he wanted to replace the historically established distance between these two nationalities with privilege. Christ died for all mankind, Jews and Gentiles alike. Peter, being somewhat skittish, was unable to stand against his strictly Jewish counterparts, and a harsh disagreement ensued. So over the years, through study and much contemplation, history has come to prove that God wanted Paul to bring liberty and promise to the Gentiles, while Peter was to preach the good news to the Jewish people. There was tension here; it was packed with emotion and a strong conviction. As well, in the situation described here, there was the obvious presence of pain. However, the impact simply had to be significant enough to initiate an investment that surpassed merely an emotional outburst. Quite similarly, the intentions of this author must be firm, as they stand against an established hierarchy, one that lacks the sensitivity and the insight necessary to bring about change—to tweak, if you will, the organized church.

The church as we have come to know it today has suffered an evolutionary downturn. Through the tension of many, some have discovered, maybe uncovered, what seems to be a protected hierarchy, a stage of sophisticated administrators who have established a new set of rules. Some have said it's the cult of celebrity, like a pop star. With sufficient track records of amassing people and talent, thereby being able to prove success, a corner has been turned. In order for the church to remain true to itself, it must allow criticism of itself and submit to a higher level of accountability, to enlist with a global network of theological testing and evaluation. It has been said that the church will continue to be teachable as we give ourselves to corrective criticism. A conclusion to such a time-tested evaluation could prove the church or find it to be a fraud. The consequences are set against the benefits, and both are eternal. While some churches are striving to find this new identity, the church has already been formed. no one needs to make new rules. We don't need to be bigger and louder and more dynamic. The things that I should anticipate in my church today were spelled out hundreds of years ago. We do not need to be relevant *with* the world by any stretch of our often secular imagination; however, we must be relevant *to* the world, which is living true to the Gospel of Jesus Christ. The church will stand on its own. It has for years and will until Christ's return. Furthermore, the idea of the church standing alone is not passive; it's a biblical posture, an assignment after putting on the full armor of Christ. It's the posture of a warrior who has spent a lifetime in preparation for this moment in time. While it may lack the flashing lights of the platform, by no means will drudgery define its work or intention.

In this chapter, we have exposed the encroachment of secularism in our theological thinking. Parishioners have been reduced to a workforce, while the clergy is in charge of conversions. Ordinary people, the undervalued, have no place other than as an economical support system, while the passionate and the creative sit idly by because they fail to fit within the scope of a one-man vision. Converts, as well, have become a product of tabulation, and it's at this point one can see that we're losing our army. Looking over our shoulders, we can see them walking away and over the hill; they're gone. Perhaps you will agree that there has been a reasonable amount of turmoil displayed in the overall assessment of my early life as a warrior within the church. As there were often times of great spiritual victory, there was also an occasional overshadowing that warned me of a tiring human element. This was a continual reminder that a warrior must be discerning, desperate, and determined in finding their way. The warrior will also come to know the sound of reward, the underlying quietness of spirit saying, "This is the way, walk ye in it" (Isaiah 30:19–22 NIV).

4

IN THE COURSE OF TIME
A HEALING OF MEMORY

One of the most relaxing things I engage in is reading. I'm not referring to the disciplined study of something deep and thought provoking. I am talking about mentally checking out, finding a book that takes me to yesterday, where building a shelter, hunting for food, or paddling a canoe up the Madison River would depict the life of a true frontiersman. And so late in the evening, I make my way to that sacred spot on my bookshelves where the right selection will be waiting for me. I've done this countless times before. From there, I go to our bedroom, close the door, and open the window just a crack to let in the cool evening air. After turning on the lamp and tucking myself in, I can hear the sounds of the night, and I settle in for an adventure. Except for the passing of an occasional car on the highway nearby, it's quite peaceful, so I make myself comfortable, slowly turn the pages, and read to my heart's content. In the background of my mind, I'm still waiting hopefully for the one thing that will make this nighttime panorama complete. Just five or six miles from our home, there's a large railway terminal where numerous times each evening comes the distant sound of an approaching train. As it travels closer, you can hear it strain, struggling to gain some momentum in the gradual upward pull. The window will rattle some, and then I can hear the entire train clicking along as it passes by, probably a mile and a half away and parallel to our home. The whistle will blow at each road crossing, and soon it's off in the distance, where all that can be heard is the occasional shrill of a whistle and the soft, deep sound of those powerful engines. Having ridden my saddle horse in the foothills above the gradual winding of the tracks, I can picture in my mind what it will look like in those wide, sweeping turns that are ahead, and I can see the brightness of the engine's headlight as it rumbles continually up the hill and into the long tunnel that awaits. Then at last, this long, cold mass of steel and cargo is gone, and the distant sounds of rumbling tracks and the dimming of a single light will turn to be a fading memory.

Oh, I nearly forgot about the book! Quite likely, it would have been about one of the Native American tribes that played such a historic role in the shaping of the west. I prefer reading about some of the tribes that were the closest to our home. I want to know them; I want to better understand how they survived the harsh winters and the battles they fought among themselves and eventually the white man. I want to know the underlying current of their culture and what makes them tick. A brief study of anthropology will only tell you that the more you learn, the more you do not know. The Native Americans themselves, having never been able to record the events of history through writing, have relied totally on memory. Similar to a passing train, it has faded into the distance, and memory holds it only as we would like to see it return. We seem to coddle these as though they were a bygone lover. As a result, much of history has been passed on to countless generations through memory, and "memory is often selective, which means that the remembered past may not always coincide with historical past" (William Shannon, president of the International Thomas Merton Society, in the introduction of Thomas Merton's *The Seven Story Mountain*, p. xxii).

Also, what's passed along with memory is where recollection coincides with interpretation, and interpretation is so often shaped by prejudice, the occasional demon in us all.

The passing of memories has consequences, all of which hold us accountable. Nonetheless, at birth, each of us was handed an unfair bill of goods, a history if you will, most of which we do not ask to be responsible for. The consequences, however, do have effects, and I, maybe like you, have a story that depicts a rather sordid past. My particular story reveals an account of facts that I did not help to create, but somehow they turned out to be a shaping mechanism that developed my inner person. True, as we become new creatures in Christ, the old is put behind us, so we're told, and "all things have become new" (Psalm 103:12 NIV). However, as we have come to trust scripture to be a faithful companion, beyond doubt, time has a way of helping us remember, to go deeper. And we should dig deeper into our recollection where we can revisit, so to speak, these hidden areas that sometimes affect us so profoundly. I continually remind myself that the walk of a Christian is forever a mystery, one where time and experiences of life open new doors of understanding to the past. They must be pursued, however, because they call us individually to their discovery. None of this is intended for us to regress in our spiritual lives; however, without question, it does begin to define a new season in our growth. Looking back, now we can begin to see patterns of behavior that have had their effects, and as we evaluate them in the light of who we intend to be before the God of heaven, there comes a demand for separation.

For me, a new season began at one time with a verse of scripture. "Forget the former things; do not dwell on the past. See, I am doing a new thing! Now it springs up; do you not perceive it? I am making a way in the desert and streams in the wasteland" (Isaiah 43:18–19 NIV). I must say there was no misunderstanding that this verse was for me. I pled with God for clarification, but it wasn't to be. This eventually brought new responsibilities and challenges, and I can honestly say that I walked with a lighter step. In time, my focus was changed, and my life with Christ somehow gained a fresh understanding. This verse became a dividing line, a new season, and then, "in the course of time," we moved to a completely different scenario.

It wasn't too much later then that my son was receiving his PhD for completed studies done in the UK. He and his wife invited us to travel with them to England for this award, and we were delighted to oblige them. Preparations were made, and we eagerly waited for this time together. As could be predicted, the suspense of such an occasion was beyond anything we had ever done previously. The official time came, however, and we were off to our agreed-upon point of rendezvous. With this being a winter flight, we were threatened, of course, with encroaching weather conditions. Having literally escaped a forecasted blizzard, we were finally in the air and headed for our destination. After we were past the borders of the continental US, we began to relax, and I became fixated with the individual seat-mounted GPS. I watched this technological wonder throughout the flight, locating landmarks and then the wide-open North Atlantic Ocean. Soon, nighttime began to fall, and the only thing that could be identified from my passenger seat window was the occasional glitter of the moon falling on the water below.

When I began to see just a glimmer of the next day's light, I noticed a connection of land and water some 35,000 feet below. Glancing at my GPS, I saw that we were flying over the English Channel. With everyone else fast asleep, I looked intently down at that great body of water, and déjà vu set in like a flood. I recalled my dad's stories of crossing the English Channel as they entered their field of operations during WWII. Suddenly, these stories became very real. I could envision those giant ships loaded with men and cargo. I could imagine then, as we crossed over England, peaking through the clouds below and visualizing the American armament all engaged in the fight of their lives against the Germans under the command of the murdering tyrant Adolph Hitler.

As is common, flights destined for England frequently connect their passengers through Frankfurt, Germany, and this was our experience. When we arrived at the airport, German guards with machine guns were everywhere, and although I thought I kept the feelings of anger to myself, apparently I showed everyone my lack of appreciation for this staunch military display. I confess that I couldn't understand my own emotions. I was angry and didn't know why. It was several years later that my son asked me about this incident. "Dad, why were you so angry in Germany?" I remembered, but I failed to understand it at all.

My father was a storyteller, and he told me of the horrors of WWII. I can recall him now telling me of crossing the English Channel. He told me about France, England, and about the bombings of Germany. He told me of the atrocities done to the Jews and showed me a little collection of bones he had gathered from an actual burial dump of slaughtered Jewish people. I can still see these in my memory. Storytellers remember things as they were seen and with the flavor they saw them. And as they tell them to others, they in turn become an agent of that storyteller. They conjure up the same hate the storyteller had. This is a hate that carefully tucks itself away, only to breed its own unforgiveness and extend discontent toward anyone and everyone who seems to cross its path. This becomes an attitude that permeates an individual's whole being. The hate that my father felt for the Germans had now become my hate. Unforgiveness of Germans for him was now unforgiveness of Germans for me. The seed of hate that was imparted to me now held no bounds; it developed into further hate and anger. Just as love, joy, and peace are from one Author, so is anger, hate, and discontent. This became a generational curse that I didn't deserve or ask for but inherited. It wasn't just an influence. Even more, it became an infection incapable of coexisting with the spiritual qualities my heavenly Father had imparted to me.

Miroslav Volf, in his book *The End Of Memory: Remembering Rightly in a Violent World,* says this:

> Now consider memories of wrongs in their passive form - memories that happen to us, rather than memories that we actively pursue. For not only do we act on memories of wrongs suffered; these memories act on us too. They steal our attention, and they assault us with inner turmoil marked by shame, guilt and maybe a mixture of self-recrimination and self-rejection. They envelop us in dark mists of melancholy, they hold us back so that we cannot project ourselves into the future and embark on new paths. They chain our identity to the injuries we have suffered and shape the way we react to others. Such memories are not just clusters of information about the past- not even clusters of information stored for the future. They themselves are powerful agents ... All of the afore holds true whether we act on memories or they act on us.

Now it was I, not my father, who was in the fight for my life. The decision to walk through this challenge and forgive was mine, and it seemed to provoke a search that moved me closer to the healing of my soul. It had become mine to forgive without reservation and to discipline my mind to be in harmony with the life and actions of the God I love and to whom I had committed my allegiance. Exposure to this generational hatred could not be tolerated, and I was crushed under the weight of it all. This was not a season of achievement or financial success; it was a season of renewal, one born out of revisiting the past. Perhaps others have found this dangerous territory, but for me, it was ground that needed to be reclaimed. It began as I kept a record of wrongs and lived by hate, the philosophy of this world. While I will never take back the opportunities once stolen or the damage of my identity from the shell of insecurity, I now had to choose for the sake of my own deliverance and lay claim to the identity of this new season. There were no limitations. It became mine to reverse the consequences of my earlier actions and gain favor and respect.

Albert White Hat was a Native American of the Lakota Sioux tribe. Like myself, he had a history where the consequences of his tribal heritage awarded him the responsibility of reclaiming his rightful identity. If you know anything of western American history, you will remember that the Lakota Sioux were followers of Sitting Bull and a proud Native American people once robbed, raped, and murdered by the United States military during the so-called settling of the west by European settlers. While listening to Albert White Hat speak, you could tell that he bore the scars of what seemed to be a generational curse. There was regret, indecision, anger, and hate. During one of his soul-searching times, he chose to go on a vision quest (a private, spiritual ceremony typical of the culture), where he would seek the mind of the Maker. It was when he left the boarding school he had attended that he recalls,

> I came out of there totally ashamed of who I am and what I am. In the late sixties I went back to the culture. On my own I let my hair grow, I started to speak my language. And in one of those times I fasted; I did the vision quest for five years. And one of those years, it was a beautiful night; the stars were out and it was calm, just beautiful. It was around midnight and I got up and I prayed. I sat down and I sat there for a while. Then all of a sudden I had flashbacks of like Sand Creek—Wounded Knee. And every policy and every law that was imposed on us by the Government and the churches hit me one at a time and how it affected my life one at a time. As I sat there I got angrier and angrier until it turned to hatred. And I looked at the whole situation, the whole picture and there was

nothing I could do, it's too much! The only thing I could do, to me, was when I came off that hill I am going to grab a gun and I am going to start shooting and go that way. Maybe then my Grandfather will honor me if I go that route. I got up and came around and faced the East and it was beautiful. It was dawn light, enough light to see the rolling hills out there. And right above that blue light, in the darkness was the sliver of the moon and the morning star. I wanted to live. I wanted to be happy. I feel I deserve it. But the only way that I was going to do that was if I forgive. And I cried that morning because I had to forgive.

Every day I work on that commitment. I don't know how many people feel it but every one of us, if you are a Lakota Sioux, you have to deal with that at some point in your life and you have to address it and you have to make a decision. If you don't you're going to die on the road someplace, either from being too drunk or you might take a gun to your head if you don't handle those situations. This isn't history, it's still with us. What has happened in the past will never leave us. Next one hundred-two hundred years it will still be with us. We have to deal with it every day.

There is a considerable amount of Native American history in this account, and if you can understand it on the level of that culture and in the particular time period he is referring to, it has the most impact. It's safe to say, however, that the message could be adjusted to fit every culture regardless of race, color, or creed. We all have a reason to be angry. I have yet to know of anyone who is left without a story of wrongs being suffered, and yet we come to a crossroad; who is going to initiate a turnaround? Albert White Hat died in the summer of 2013. By looking at his internet activity, it becomes obvious that he made the right choice, resulting in a positive impact on the Lakota Sioux people. He was able to teach the Lakota language to many of his people, and through his leadership, an alphabet was developed whereby the language can now be written and read as well. White Hat was instrumental in constructing the proper native vocabulary for the Kevin Costner movie *Dances with Wolves*. Without knowing White Hat personally, it would be entirely impossible to even guess at his belief system, except that it is definitely of the Lakota Sioux dialect. Regardless, he put forgiveness at the very center of his belief, realizing that hate is destructive, while love overcomes and builds relational bridges. Mr. White Hat and I would agree on one very vital ingredient to living a forgiving life; he said straightforwardly, "Every day I have to work on that commitment." And my own experience teaches me that under certain stressful experiences in life and business, I can again be the man I don't want to be; it's a choice, and I must continue to forgive.

> In our world of loneliness and despair, there is an enormous need for men and women who know the heart of God, a heart that forgives, that cares, that reaches out and wants to heal. In that heart there is no superstition, no vindictiveness, no resentment and no tinge of hatred. It is a heart that wants to give and love and receive love in response. It is a heart that suffers immensely because it sees the magnitude of human pain and the great resistance to trusting the heart of God who wants to offer consultation and hope. (Henri J.M. Nouwen, *In the Name of Jesus*)

Just recently, having returned from some traveling, my wife and I met with our extended family for an evening out. We chose to go to a restaurant we had frequented and found ourselves sitting next to a Native American family who was enjoying family time as well. Our table was actually quite close to theirs, so to excuse myself as I passed between the tables, I casually made a comment to the little girl. "Could I share one of your french fries?" And she was quick to say in her timid voice, "No." I smiled and assured her that she had made a good choice. After all, I was a perfect stranger.

After we finished our meal, I approached the little girl's mother, hoping I hadn't offended her or the family. This woman smiled when she said that immediately after I was denied the french fry, the little girl's older brother told her, "Mom, he should have been given a french fry; he's a papa." Someone within his school of learning had taught him that the seniors among us should be shown special honor. This young man had learned his lessons well. What they had not taught him, however, was the difference between ethnicities. He was unable to discern with prejudice the difference between his people and my people. His actions were pure, undefiled, and in total respect and consideration. Seemingly, the wall of generational hatred had been demolished, and love and respect had constructed a new bridge. Skin color and the features of nationality had paled and, in the course of time, had opened a space for the possibilities of friendship and mutual compatibility.

5

AT THE FENCE LINE

Not by might nor by power.
—Zachariah 4:6 (NIV)

In the language of my neighboring Crow Indians, it was in the moon when the leaves are on the ground, November. It was a cold and snowy Saturday, and a friend and I agreed to travel a short distance into the countryside for some afternoon deer hunting. The place we had selected was located near numerous patches of wooded hills that were scattered across the open prairie, so typical of southcentral Montana. Each of us took a backpack that contained everything a good hunter would need to ensure survival regardless of the situation. After all, with the right equipment, you are never lost; you may just have to hunker down in a quickly made shelter with a small fire and make do for the night. So after finding a location that held promise, we drove slowly down a gravel road to a place that suggested we take a closer look. This was exciting, a grove of trees not too far off the road with some hills and small drainages that held promise for whitetail or mule deer. Immediately after leaving the vehicle, we split up, with the idea of meeting back at the pickup in an hour or so. And because we simply wanted to look over the next ridge, neither of us took our backpacks.

Not long after we parted company, I spotted some mule deer at a distance and began my stalk. Not actually having much interest in what I saw, I knew there could potentially be other sizable bucks within the close proximity of this bunch. I poked around for a while, going into deep ravines and up steep hillsides, through bunched-up trees and then the open prairie, but the deer were gone. Without any question as to my whereabouts, I felt that my direction had gradually turned me back toward the pickup. There was no sun to help me, as a winter storm was in the immediate forecast, and in fact light snow was beginning now to cover my tracks. I began to see things I hadn't recalled seeing when I entered this no-man's-land, and the road that was supposed to be just over the next hill somehow wasn't there. Without getting too excited, I called my friend on the cell phone to ask if he would honk the horn in his pickup so I could get my bearings. He did so, and not only was his horn blast silent in my part of the wilderness, but my phone warned me that the battery was near dead as well.

As I walked, I suddenly remembered that I had a compass clipped to my jacket zipper, only to find that it had fallen out. And to make matters progressively worse, I had also started to sweat—a bad thing to do in a survival situation—and the reality of becoming dehydrated hit me at the same time. Darkness was falling fast, and the intensity of the snowfall was increasing. I finally had to confess to myself that I was lost, and everything that I didn't want to happen was happening. By this time, I had been gone over three hours, and the snow had covered my tracks completely. I was hungry, thirsty, and sweating, and the concern of hypothermia continued to taunt me. Although I was never overcome with fear, the thought of someone finding me frozen to the ground by the next day's light was real. Eventually, I came to a fence and stopped. I had no idea which way to go, so I leaned my rifle against a post and began to pray. It was a resignation of sorts. I honestly felt that life for me was over, and what little time remained would be difficult to experience. I was played out. As I had sensed the Lord's very presence throughout this ordeal, my conversation with him was sweet: "Father God, only you know where I am and what my present condition is. I've come to realize that I am totally dependent on you at this point, and unless you provide a way, I won't make it through the night. I am so happy to say that I am yours and you are mine, and by the way, when I cross this fence, should I go left, right, or straight ahead? Amen."

Those in competitive sports would call this hitting the wall. What it amounts to is you are spent and can do no more. In some cases, this could be called a psychological breakdown or spiritual exhaustion. Any and all of an individual's resources have either been used up or, similar to my experience, left back at the vehicle. Our decision-making process fails us in conditions of this nature, and we beg for rescue, which if it were left to our own reasoning would mean to be reinstated with things being just as they were before this very dilemma of our lives. If we listen, however, past our temporal need of rescue, we can gain wisdom and grasp a deeper understanding for the purposes of tomorrow and the sake of the kingdom. This is not a midlife evaluation; it's intended to challenge our mindset.

Back at the fence line, reasoning and better judgment were no longer an option for me. It became a matter of total trust. After crossing the fence, I took hold of my firearm, and although fully intending to go to the right, my feet took me straight ahead … and I was totally aware of what happened. Then, seeing a hillside at a distance, I set my direction toward it so as not to go in a circle. Soon afterward, I got sight of what looked to be an abandoned implement shed. After viewing it through my field glasses, I was comforted to see that it could at least be a shelter from the wind and snow. As I approached this building, I noticed that just beyond stood an old, deserted farmhouse, and now the thought of a woodstove with some thoughtfully placed matches began to cheer me up. Believe me, this was still a long way from hot cocoa and marshmallows, but there was a flicker of hope. Eventually, from this old farmhouse, I found my way to the county road, and then a working farm, a phone, and finally my rescue. That day, I died, quite literally, to the life I had known. There was not one thing that I could do for my own rescue; there was no going back to the way things were before. All I could do was humbly acknowledge what happened and give myself, through abandonment, to a plan much greater than my own.

When a breakdown experience shows itself, the thought generally is to regroup and get back on track. But when we stand before God at a time as serious as the illustration I have shown here, the worst thing we can do is draw upon our own resources or to reengage in the same way or at the same pace as before. So often, we are challenged by experiences that could be terrifying, and yet in the storm of our lostness, we fail to recognize the hand of God at work. We become desperate, we panic, and we allow our particular temperament or personality free rein. Worst of all, we fail to listen beyond our temporal need of rescue. These are platforms for new performance, and as warriors, we truly must discern the defining need. Here, there is pain because in order to experience the elixir of life, one may need to deny all established prominence and existing resources, only to stand at the fence line and humbly ask the way. I've heard of too many leaders and read too many authors who rely on intellect, experience, or established profile and haven't enough pain. There is also the possibility that the pain that has been or is being experienced is misappropriated. Through self-evaluation or even counseling, the endeavor is to regain status or reestablish a foothold so as to continue on in the same vein rather than experience a new vision. Consequently, their message and their writing have no value. It's of human origin; it's empty. And the same applies to the Christian businessman. The only way to reestablish one's self is to yield to the pain, and you will in effect be found. The elixir demands the unconditional consent of the heart.

That all being said, the two most prominent enemies of our souls are the intellect and our resources. Don't misunderstand; the intellect is a valuable asset. However, in God's economy, it, along with reasoning and better judgment, comes second. And when an organization or an individual has resources, they can leverage a project or a program; however, there is nothing worse than wood, hay, or stubble. While God can and certainly does use certain resources, it has become obvious to me that God can and will provide them. These potential enemies are also bedfellows, couched alongside cowardice and fear; they rob one of creativity and resign to the stale overtones of doing things conventionally. Together, these adversaries will keep one at status quo when the possibility of something fresh, initiated by Creator God, will defeat these enemies and score victoriously for the kingdom.

The few words that make up this chapter's subtitle are curious. To put it bluntly, they are not the words that would be found in the how-to of any business troubleshooting catalog. They totally defy today's modern methods of administrative instruction. Of course, we would encourage the use of physical and mechanical strength to turn the gears of production, especially in the case of a building project. How else could one manage to get things accomplished? These simple words that were given to the prophet Zechariah were part of an instruction process, a manual if you will, for reconstruction, not only of a building but of a defeated people who had suffered foreign captivity. Although we're not in the process of rebuilding a temple, the message should apply to the methods by which we go about our affairs. Not forgetting the thought of this chapter, being at the fence line of our lives, the people of Zechariah's time were at a dead end as well. However, through a series of visions, the message became clear: the light of God's church will burn with ever-flaming brightness, for it is not by might (physical strength) or by power (mechanical strength) but by the Spirit.

Divine Disposition and Courage

God told his people through Zechariah what he longs to tell each of us. At the admission of our lostness, he wants us to experience him in a new and unique way. He literally told his people that they would be a safe community even without a wall surrounding the city; he was going to be that wall! Make no mistake. Security, the dependence of our stored-up energy and resources, is an idol; we are never at our best for Christ when we depend on ourselves for anything. We must learn to trust. However, this becomes a dividing line in which some, in order to follow Christ, must turn their backs on the power and prestige they have depended on for so long. This is where a *divine dispos*ition, our frame of mind, coupled with courage, thinks and plans differently. Henri Nouwen was a Catholic priest who spent twenty years in the academic world as a teacher of pastoral psychology, pastoral theology, and Christian spirituality. At one point in his career, he began to experience a deep inner threat.

> Everyone was saying that I was doing really well, but something inside me was telling me that my success was putting my soul in danger. It was very hard for me to see clearly and I woke up one day with the realization that I was living in a very dark place and that the term "burnout" was a convenient psychological translation for a spiritual death. (*In the Name of Jesus*, p.10)

During this time of lostness, his continual prayer was "Lord, show me where you want me to go, and I will follow you." Within a very short time, the opportunity showed itself in the form of being a chaplain of a school for the mentally challenged. Wow, from the brightest, a professor at Harvard, to a priest to the mentally handicapped at L'Arche (Daybreak, the L'Arche community in Toronto). We cannot forget what was said earlier, "If we listen, however, past our temporal need of rescue we can gain wisdom and grasp a deeper understanding for the purposes of tomorrow and the sake of the Kingdom."

To understand Nouwen's thought process, we must follow his devotional life. As his motivation, he had taken literally the lessons of Peter recorded in the book of John.

> Now we have to turn to Jesus again because, after having asked Peter three times if he loved him more than the others and after having commissioned him three times to be a shepherd, he said in a very emphatic way: "In all truth I tell you, when you were young you put on your belt and walked where you liked; but when you grow old you will stretch out your hands and somebody else will put a belt around you and take you where you would rather not go." (John 21:18 NIV)

> These words made it possible for me to move from Harvard to L'Arche. They touch the core of Christian leadership and are spoken to offer us ever and again new ways to let go of power and follow the humble way of Jesus. But Jesus has a different vision of maturity: It is the ability and willingness to be led where you would rather not go. Immediately after Peter has been commissioned to be a leader of his sheep, Jesus confronts him with the hard truth that the servant-leader is the leader who is being led to unknown, undesirable, and painful places. The way of the Christian leader might not be the way of upward mobility in which the world has invested so much, but the way of downward mobility ending at the cross.

There are three things that strike me here as most important while considering the divine disposition and courage of Henri Nouwen: there was a strong sensitivity within, a heart that had been carefully cultivated to discern the difference between true godly success and self-aggrandizement, while allowing only one to be on the throne of his life. Most will agree that this would then demand a very disciplined course of action; power and prestige are strong attractions and can be an addiction. Secondly, he maintained a continuous attitude of prayer as he sought other fulfilling options. This can take time. When we spend time alone with God on concerns of this magnitude, our mind and emotions generally need a new focus, maybe a complete overhaul because we must see things as he sees them. No one can say when or how God might speak to an individual. I would say even with our best intentions or as spiritually centered as we think they may be, our time in constant prayer is paramount. And thirdly, he searched the scriptures to find examples and illustrations by which he could check his own direction. There is a rhythm to scripture. You don't understand or recognize it by going to it on occasion; it's by continual and repetitious feeding, by learning that it is the very life breath of a Christ follower. When I have been away from it for a few days, it begs my heart for only a glimpse to be once again washed by the water of its words. Counsel, even with the best of persons, can at times be misleading; however, Mr. Nouwen was aware of the needs of his soul, while reasoning and better judgment, as previously mentioned, took second place.

Divine Vigor and Vivacity

Each of the divine attributes listed above describes an attitude of the heart. They aren't from a defeatist position; they understand in any situation, lost or abandoned, that God is in control and there is always hope. And when we pray, are we allowing God to change us to fit the picture he has in mind, or do we use prayer subconsciously to manipulate a plan of our own? Would confession play any part at all in being found? The tendency here might be for some to think that this would only apply to church leaders in order to affect the community; however, each of us, regardless of our position in the affairs of homemaking, commerce, or trade, is the church, and the part we play in community or home does make a statement as to the strength of the church in a lost world, for which we are accountable.

Caleb is one of many biblical heroes. Selected by Moses from the established tribal leadership, he and eleven other men were chosen to spy out a land that God had intended for his chosen people to inhabit. For those of us who are students of scripture and have read this account over and again, I seriously wonder if we get it. This was land that promised to be filled with milk and honey—in other words. the best of everything. However, these spies soon discovered that the present inhabitants were giants, and fear struck their hearts. Upon their return, they brought some of the luscious produce of the land to show the people, but ten of the twelve spies trembled with fear. "These are giants," they said. "We could never defeat these people." But God wasn't asking his people to do anything except admit their inadequacy and allow him to do something through them. He was asking them to move straight toward their greatest fear. Long story short, because of their fear and the poor decision that followed, the children of Israel were never allowed to go into the land that God had promised them, and a complete generation was lost due to disobedience and unbelief. However, God did reward both Joshua and Caleb for their strong faith. Not only were their lives spared, but Joshua took the challenge to follow Moses as the new leader of God's chosen people, and then when Caleb was eighty-three years of age, the subject of his obedient faith was again brought to the forefront. Caleb once again said that he was as strong as ever and was prepared to take the challenge and fight for his inheritance. Recognizing that opportunity had knocked at the door of his tent, he said enthusiastically, "Give me this mountain!" This was the response of an elderly, seasoned man of God, a true warrior of the faith.

I have a friend who is elderly as well. Over the past few years, some of his family, through drug use and trafficking, lost their three children to the state's legal system. It was then and in this peculiar way that opportunity, similar to that of Caleb, came to my friend as well. Although this wasn't a glamorous challenge, heaven was watching out for these children, and the state offered them to these grandparents. As a result, three beautiful kids now live with my friend and his wife, and it has challenged them beyond belief. It's an uphill journey. This is far from how they imagined they would spend their supposed glory years, but they are impacting these children, and the kingdom will be the beneficiary. The choice was theirs; they could slump in their couch in front of CNN every night or scrub little butts before bedtime. They chose the latter. Later it will be remembered that an elderly couple chose to be endowed with a divine vigor and vivacity, and three children are privileged to experience love and organization, clean sheets, a bedtime story, and prayer every night. Life had never been like that before. My friend was challenged by one of the very necessities of life, and he, like Caleb, was willing to accept that challenge. Interestingly enough, warriors don't choose their assigned place of service; their only choice is in obedience, which is followed immediately by the God of the universe, who reaches out to take us by the hand.

Divine Life and Animation

As you may guess, the story of my hunting trip has been rehearsed time and again. The lessons continue to speak to me with clarity. What I have discovered are some thoughts that have been lifetime lessons, only now to be lived out. To begin with, my experience on the cold, deserted prairie followed a two-year period of no employment. Our family-owned business went through a slump that was not typical for my trade in our part of the country. My competitors were swamped with work, and over this extended time, I bid job after job only to find continued disappointment. Remembering that I had always wanted to author a book, I simply began that work in spite of our situation. My own reasoning would have told me that this would not have been the right time, and believe me, it was difficult to do while not abandoning my post. I stuck with it, however, for two years, and it was in the month of November that my publisher gave me the word that in December my first book would print. I was ecstatic; however, during this desperate time of no employment, we sold numerous vehicles and other pieces of equipment. Our business family refinanced our personal homes and began to purchase even our groceries on the card. Needless to say, things were strenuous, and we went to bed each night with aches in our chests. As this time was spent in financial loss and pain, we committed ourselves to the Lord, for what his intentions were for us, and then finally one day, things began to change. The phone began to ring, and jobs began to fall into place. These were jobs that were profitable, and we gained a work momentum that had never been ours previously. It was at this time that I went on the infamous hunting trip mentioned. What developed from that experience was phenomenal to say the least. I began to experience a new way of doing business, a new way of customer consultation and bidding, and consequently, a new profile began to establish itself and has proven to be a profitable learning process.

I'm not the same person I was back then, as many things have changed. There is no regret for having walked straight forward when my intentions had been to go to the right. And there has been no regret for allowing God to alter my course in business or Christian ministry. The direction that my wife and I have taken regarding church attendance was challenged as well in the most unusual of ways. We have spoken of this change on many occasions and have only good to say of the results, not to mention the enlightenment of this altered course.

Again, there are several things that strike me as most important while looking through the microscope at my experience. To begin with, I, like Henry Neuwin, acknowledged my lostness, I agreed to it with God at the fence line, and then and most importantly, I moved forward. I realize that to keep moving in a snowstorm on the prairie wasn't the wisest thing to do, but had I stayed put, I undoubtedly would have frozen to the ground. As always, it has been my experience with God to move forward in the light that you have, and you will find rescue.

By Divine Executive Ability and Technical Skill

In today's economy, it's a specialist that's in demand in every area of our lives. A specialist is one who has devoted his or her attention to one or a few select areas of a specific job as their expertise. They've dedicated enormous amounts of time and educated energy to develop the best way of doing a specific thing. Facetiously, it's been said that a specialist is the average guy from another town; in other words, we consider this person above the ordinary. Categorically, a specialist would be an individual with technical skills or an executive ability. However, executives and technicians are not a select group in the hierarchy of anything; they are normal people who like their job and have excelled in it. To put it in a language that some might better understand, an executive might be the guy who gives direction to a staff of underlings, but he couldn't change a flat tire. He or she might wear a suit and command a staff of people all toward one main objective, and they may or may not be highly educated, only highly skilled. As I have taken my job quite seriously, I have become an executive, one with a divine ability. And most importantly, when I look good to the world, I look good for Jesus, and the church is stronger for it.

So what does it mean to have a divine ability? So many of the affairs of our lives today are dictated by our social structure. The media, through television and radio, influences us on a continual basis; this is how you should structure your financial affairs, this is the way you plan for the future, this is how you set up for retirement. Quite literally, the homes we live in, the automobiles we drive, and the way we dress ourselves are dictated by social media. So we strive for these things not only in providing for ourselves but in how we dictate our positions of life, our investments, and our future. Eventually, these desires consume us and rob our hearts of the tender way in which God longs to direct us. So in answer to the leading question, what does it mean to have a divine ability, *strife* is the word that describes the exact contrast. When you find that strife defines your work and your ambitions, or your relationships, or a project, then you are not being guided by the Holy Spirit of God. There will be things you must possess to be successful when you have the eyes of the world, and you will strive to secure them. There will be things that present themselves as a security for the future, and so you strive to put them in place even at the expense of evenings away from home and weekend work. They become an idol; they set themselves up against God's natural laws. In contrast, God knows what we will need for the future, and he longs to provide it; however, *trust* is the key to any divine activity. All of our battles and all of our lost times belong to the Lord.

It's not that God wants to deprive us of the things that bring pleasure or having a little nest egg so that one day we might not have to be as ambitious as when we are young. God wants to provide these things, but from my experience, I have come to believe that what God really wants is more of me. At one time in my life, I became continually reminded of a sensitive area that needed to be abandoned to Christ. Although this became very painful for me, I dealt with it, and now the resulting memory of this seems to surface when I see someone striving to get what he or she thinks they desire or deserve out of life. For me, it's easy to discern that God is asking that person for something they have tucked away in the back of their mind; it's their secret. And they quite likely lack a full and complete abandonment to God in this area. So they run, and each time God asks to talk to them about it, each time he whispers in their heart about that secret, they turn away. And one day, he will not ask anymore because he refuses to pry his way into our hearts. The cost will be in experiencing a lack of freedom, resulting in a stale testimony, no real fruit bearing, and consequently, the church is weakened all because of our own cowardly will. The *divine abilities* are about lordship. It's been said that if Christ isn't lord of all, then he's not lord at all.

As Christians, we have been taught to believe that living somewhat upright, attending church services regularly, and engaging in a reasonable devotional life are all that's required of us. Personally, I have found this insufficient and unfulfilling. It's seldom that I could talk to an individual at any length not to discover that there is something or someone who, when brought to mind, continues to pester them. It's these that beg our attention at the fence line of our lives. When will we finally yield this troubled area for a true heavenly examination? The humdrum of life and business become the attraction, whereas quietly, the voice within us tries to divert that attention toward an objective that could prove effective for the kingdom. These will arrest our normal lifestyle and provoke our curiosity. This is the stuff of Joshua and Caleb, Henri Nouwen, and others who, through this type of spiritual engagement, found freedom and began to really minister to others. Outside of this, we are nothing, and the words of the song writer come to haunt me: "I'm just a whisper of smoke, I'm just a shadow upon these walls." Life isn't about our financial portfolio or our retirement; it's about something far greater and has more significance. It's about our obedience and listening to the God of our existence, the God of Abraham, Moses, and Daniel, to mention a few. These became warriors because they were able to hear God call them and then, through faith, rise to the challenge and become the warriors of their time. (See Hebrews 11.) What Jesus once said to his disciples, he said to each of us, "If anyone would come after me, he must deny himself and take up his cross daily and follow me. For whoever wants to save his life will lose it, but whoever loses his life for me will save it. What good is it for a man to gain the whole world and yet lose or forfeit his very self" (Matthew 9:23–25 NIV).

6

FOR SUCH A TIME AS THIS

*For if you remain silent at this time, relief and deliverance
will arise from another place.*
—Esther 4:14a (NIV), paraphrased

Authors have at times made our country's natives out to be nothing other than beggars and thieves, but make no mistake they were warriors in a very real sense. Of course, today we can only see them through the confined lens of a filmmaker's camera, where he is portrayed in colorful war paint, and his mount shares the color and creativity of its owner. While this is quite picturesque in real life, it only fits the limited white American idea. The tribal people of the plains were contenders. They survived only because they fought for everything they ever had or did. The threat of mere existence permeated the very fiber of their beings; they chased the roaming buffalo, moved incessantly to find food, and warred frequently over territory and privilege. They understood that their lives were forever in danger, and survival was a continual battle. There was no day when life was casual; it was desperate, intentional, and in complete contrast with the lifestyle we share today.

The American Indian of the plains understood one thing that the church of today believes in but fails to comprehend: there is an adversary. Along with this knowledge, instilled in the native from birth, there came a need to arm themselves with weaponry and a discipline of action that enabled them to combat whatever evil force might confront them. This became a lifetime call to vigilance—being on the lookout for danger.

And although they couldn't articulate circumspect, they lived it, looking around on all sides watchfully.

Discreetly placed and nearly hidden, one might say, in the early pages of the Old Testament is the wonderful story of Esther. Found in the book titled after her own name are ten brief chapters that chronicle in detail her heroic Jewish life. While we so often ascribe the activity of a warrior to men, as we shall see, nothing could be further from the truth. The story of Esther is one of boldness and bravery, and it reveals an important time in the lives of the Jewish people throughout the Persian Empire. We shouldn't be surprised that a government would attempt to eliminate an entire human race of people, but similar to our country's natives of little over a century ago, people and governments took their positions, and the stage was set.

King Xerxes was on the throne during Esther's time, and in the third year of his reign, he sponsored a great exhibition. The scriptures say that it was a 180-day display of wine, women, and wealth. When the party was finally at its end, the king hosted an elaborate feast that lasted for seven days. It was then, on this last day, the king, being in high spirits, decided to show Queen Vashti to his guests, and she refused to oblige him. As a result, the queen, having publicly defied the king's authority, was banned from his presence and eventually placed in isolation—forever. Following this radical expulsion, a rather intense search was conducted for a replacement of the queen, and upon finding success, an elaborate preparation time for numerous beautiful, young candidates ensued. Esther was taken into this harem of likely candidates, and without any choice in the matter, she became one of the challenging contenders.

Esther's cousin, Mordecai, raised her from childhood after the passing of both her parents, and even now he kept a watchful eye on her. Not only was Mordecai interested in Esther's every move, but he was also being supernaturally positioned in this historic panorama. One day while sitting by the king's gate, he overheard a conversation between two disgruntled guards who were planning to assassinate King Xerxes. He reported the incident, and after it was proven to be true, the guards were both hanged. Although credit was given to Mordecai for saving the king's life, nothing meritorious was done about it. Meanwhile, regular contact was in place between Esther and Mordecai, similar to the ongoing, behind-the-scenes activity of a modern-day soap opera.

When at last the time had finally arrived for Esther to go before the king, the drum roll of heaven began. It had to be that way, as heaven alone knew what lay in the near future; that is to say, no one on earth had a clue. So, with heaven's knowledge of what was to transpire, tremendous energy was being focused on the success of one orphan girl. As the drum roll continued, this stunningly gorgeous young woman walked toward the king. The projector clicked along in slow motion, and Esther, who chose not to take anything with her as a psychological crutch, walked before the penetrating scrutiny of royalty and guests alike. Her heart was pounding in her chest, and yet she was poised and confident, lacking nothing while she glanced across the room to gain the eye contact of His Majesty. The king looked intently at her, and although he saw her beauty, there was something more. Was it maturity, quietness, an inner self that reflected the passionate desire for which he longed? "And Esther won the favor of everyone who saw her" (Esther 2:17 NIV). Heaven went crazy with applause, the king was delightfully satisfied, and everything seemed right in a world that had seemingly lost all composure.

As we all know, every story has a villain, and every villain has an agenda. That being said, a man named Haman, a hater of the Jews and the second to the throne, had plotted to have the Jews throughout the entire kingdom annihilated. With this threat firmly in place, Mordecai challenged Esther to appeal to the king and change what, by all rights, could not be changed. He told Esther that the timely purpose of her position was likely to alter the course of history; "and who knows but that you have come to royal position for such a time as this" (Esther 4:14 NIV). So knowing that one mistake would mean her execution, Esther summoned her ancestors, the Jewish people everywhere, to fast and pray. "When this is done," she said, "I will go to the King, even though it is against the law. And if I perish, I perish" (Esther 4:15–16 NIV).

This is an event! At this point, wicked Haman had been given the official stamp of approval to wipe out the entire Jewish race of people. An official notice had been issued and sent throughout the land. It was as if the drum roll hadn't ended, and fear had seized the hearts of thousands of men, women, and children throughout the land. Now Esther enters the king's chamber knowing that, because she has not been formally invited, he can reject her, which would mean her execution. Once again, heaven is standing perfectly still, the drum roll is intensified, and it's as if Esther's heart and her feet are connected, one tender heart beat and one careful foot in front of the other. As the slow-motion cinema continues, we see that King Xerxes not only recognizes Esther in the chamber, but he also welcomes her with the honor of half of his kingdom. Over the next two days, things change drastically.

Miraculously, God honored the prayers of a nation; the Jewish people were spared, and Queen Esther was held in even higher esteem. Mordecai was given the position vacated by wicked Haman, who was hanged on his own preconstructed gallows, and now Mordecai became second only to the king. As history records this dramatic rescue, we scrutinize it so as to identify the key players or to possibly get a better handle on the entire story. We soon discover this isn't about Esther or Mordecai, nor is it about King Xerxes or the Persian Empire. Some might wonder if it's about a nation of people God intended to rescue, and in my mind, it was without a doubt God's providential care for his people. However, to gain further insight, we should intensify our examination of the Jewish (in our time, the Christian) defense mechanism. One can easily see some key truths here that typify warrior behavior, and after looking closer, they can also be identified as indispensable principles of the Christian faith. I have selected several of these truths for consideration as we contemplate the investment of our lives as contenders of the faith.

For some, it might be difficult to understand that everyone has an adversary. Earlier in the chapter, we spoke about those who were the first to live on American soil, the Indians. We gave credit to the fact that they were warriors and that they fought for life itself, so the question could be asked, who was their enemy? And the answer is easily discovered—other Indians, their closest neighbors, the white man, civilization, anyone or anything that threatened their lifestyle. Everyone has an adversary! The fact of this puts us all in one of two categories: those who can recognize their adversary and those who fail to see who their adversaries really are. Our company's bookkeeper was sharing a story with me recently that took us to a social issue, one that made her very upset—angry! My answer to her, after sharing the story of Esther, was that maybe this is an adversary of yours, your "wicked Haman." And if so, maybe this is your place to affect the world with the power of prayer, because as a Christian, it certainly isn't the time or place to be ugly. Esther and her people prayed. They heavily engaged in a combative, nonmilitary confrontation and won a serious battle. Prayer is not passive. It's warfare. It's an attack against evil. This in no way gives license for the Christian individual or community to pick a pet-peeve and give full expression to a carnal or vengeful attack. Instead, it becomes God's by initiation, God's by design, and God's by employment, thereby displaying a stark contrast between the warrior of yesterday and a true Christ follower.

God's by Initiation

At one time, I was part of a men's group fellowship that was stimulating to watch. These guys were learning and growing in their faith. Every week as I drove out in the country where we met, I passed a strip club that was beside a small-town truck stop. It occurred to me to start praying for that establishment, and then I thought I would ask the guys from the study to join me. Immediately, I was checked. This is a great way to attack the enemy's turf and get bruised and beaten. This is not mine to design or assign. It wasn't long after I began praying on a personal level that one of the other guys mentioned the club in a casual conversation, and I sensed that God was doing something unusual. As I continued to be prayerfully sensitive, I initiated a conversation with the men that invited their thoughts about weekly prayer for this establishment and those who worked there. The idea took hold, and then I became curious as to how they might pray. Would they ask the Lord to burn the establishment down, or would they want the law to change so it would close? Then we began. These guys prayed for the bartender, they prayed for the girls who hustled drinks, they prayed for the strippers, and they included the truck drivers who frequented this establishment. These men had compassion, and I was amazed. This was not a project; they prayed for people, a people in need of a divine infusion. These guys coupled their aggressive prayer with kindness and compassion. It wasn't long before one of the men, having visited this club prior to becoming a Christ follower, came to announce that the week earlier, he had seen one of the strippers attending the church where he was a member. He recognized her from days gone by. This nightclub was an adversary; it threatened the community with evil, and a watch was set. This was all the result of God's idea, using God's people and doing business in God's way.

God's by Design

In our supposed modern times, many fail to believe that the devil and his cohorts still toy with our lives on a regular basis. How does this happen? How can we recognize these attacks, whether subtle or aggressive? And when they do occur, what can we do about it? To begin with, not every challenging event is of the enemy in the spirit world, and even when they are, some just happen to be more intense than others. Fear itself is just one indication that our enemy, the devil, has a hand in our affairs. "For God has not given us the Spirit of fear but of power, of love and of a sound mind" (2 Timothy 1:7 KJV). In God's intricate design for his people, scripture will always help us with a clear indication and a firm guideline when we discern an enemy spirit. One afternoon after I brought my wife home from a short stay at the hospital, we had an unusual experience. Although she just had a minor surgery, it was life threatening, and while we tried to be calm about this, beneath the surface, there was concern. As soon as I got her settled in the house, she suggested that I run into town to pick up a sandwich for us both. On my return trip, short as it was, I got to the top of a hill nearby, and fear came over me like a flood. *What if this is the beginning of the end? What if . . .* You get the idea. This hill, by the way, is approximately three minutes from our house. When I arrived at home, my wife was in a recliner, crying and scared to death. I talked to her briefly about the fear she was experiencing and asked her when she began to feel this way. She said just three minutes ago! Hmmm. There are times when we need to be reminded that there really is a live enemy. We prayed against this force of evil, and the fear left us; however, scripture was the convincing and confirming factor in our discernment.

The conversation that God had with Joshua when he assumed the leadership of the children of Israel was a strict reminder to pay attention to the very first blueprint ever made:

> Do not let this Book of the Law depart from your mouth; meditate on it day and night, so that thou you may be careful to do everything written in it. Then you will be prosperous and successful. Have I not commanded you? Be strong and courageous. Do not be terrified; do not

be discouraged, for the Lord your God will be with you wherever you go. (Joshua 1:8–9 NIV)

To reread the story of Esther, it's easy to see that fear was a prominent and wicked force that presented itself. However, it became the vigilance and circumspect behavior that made it possible to set a counterattack, which of course is relying on our most prominent weapon, prayer. At one time while we were doing a multimillion-dollar building project, I began to see a tension that was very subtle, but it seemed to encroach on the overall leadership of this project. For several days, a specific word came to mind, and it rattled around in my head as if to taunt me. It would start early in the morning when I would have my coffee and reading time, and then continue throughout the day, until one morning when I got in my pickup, the thought of this word seemed to scream at me twice. At this point, I felt blindsided, completely blown away by what was about to transpire. So I started my truck and went to my phone to see what the dictionary had to say about this word, as I had no idea of its meaning. The word was *subterfuge.* "A deceptive device or stratagem, the use of cleaver underhanded actions to achieve an end, to superimpose one image on another, to create a false reality." To put it in layman terms, it would be for an individual or individuals—a faction—to look good at the expense of someone else, for the purpose of gaining leverage for control or prominence. I immediately set a watch! I told my business family, and we prayed. Actually, there were three people who worked together who had the ability to undermine a project. They had a turf to maintain, and at the expense of others, they would do whatever necessary to get it done. These three entertained what is known as *familiar spirits.* Two of them were controllers, while the third was, and had been, their puppet for many years. You don't fight these people; like Esther, you set a watch!

In my mind, this was about the most preposterous thing I had ever experienced, that God would speak into my mind with a word that defined a literal enemy of the spirit world and to set a watch. But why should we not think this way? In 2 Chronicles 20:1–24 (NIV), there is the story of an incredible battle. All God wanted his people to do was show up at their field of operations, and when they were obedient to that call, to their utter amazement, the entire enemy lay dead before their very eyes. God simply told them, "The battle is not yours but God's." The connection here is one of transition; the prophet Jeremiah records some interesting words of God himself; "Am I a God nearby," declares the Lord, "and not a God far away?" (Jeremiah 23:23 NIV). Here in this little passage, God makes it very clear that he transcends space, so why would he not transcend time, when he is "the same yesterday, today and forever" (Hebrews 13:8 NIV)? If God chose to help his people in this supernatural way of years gone by, could he not surprise us with protection in an unanticipated form today? As Christians, we cannot afford to place a parameter around our experience. A strategy that's used for any warfare is the element of surprise, and we would be wise to allow God to assist us with that element. Understand, wicked spirits infect people, programs, and projects. Our weapon of choice will be prayer and with the all-powerful name of Jesus. Caution: other than in prayer, you never wage war against a wicked spirit without taking it before a qualified and godly exorcist.

"God's by Design" is more extensive than the other two subtitles because *design* follows the principles of holy writ. Interestingly enough, these principles aren't all numbered in a column; they are tucked away in stories, such as in the one above, where they are expected to be a vital part of our everyday stuff. We would do ourselves a great inadequacy if we went completely through this heartwarming story of Esther and failed to highlight the fasting aspect of her challenge to the entire Jewish community. "Go and gather all the Jews who are in Susa and fast for me. Do not eat or drink for three days, night or day. I and my maids will fast as you do. When this is done, I will go to the King, even though it is against the law. And if I perish, I perish" (Esther 5:16 NIV). This is intense. It's final. A fast denies the body of the normal luxuries in order for oneself to give total focus on an objective before heaven. Jesus gave instruction to someone in the New Testament when they had confronted an evil spirit. He said, "This kind will only come by much fasting and prayer" (Matthew 17:21 KJV). He also said in his final instruction to his disciples, "When you fast," making the bold assumption that when we pray, which we should be doing often (always), we should also fast. It's often done by eliminating a mealtime or dedicating a specific time, maybe even with others, when we deny ourselves of what could be considered everyday luxuries, like food, and give ourselves to prayer. I will venture to say that this is not stressed as important today, as it was intended for the early church in order to be a strong influence in the world in which we live.

God's by Employment

As much as I love the study of history, I have to force myself to understand that I am living history future, and if I do nothing about the circumstances around me, I will literally unleash the enemy around me. If we profess to be contenders of the faith, there must be a counterattack. When I spoke to our bookkeeper, I was quick to tell her that when these situations come to us, we must *own them*. These challenges are ours, and the weapons of our faith must be employed. The world is full of adversaries, and we are a citizenship, an army of God that contends. We must fight for survival. The time is now. This is the future. There is no day when life is casual; in fact, life must be intentional.

While riding my saddle horse on a ranch in southcentral Montana, I was introduced to some long, vertical scars on the side of a sandstone cliff near a ranch house. The owners of the ranch said that these scars were from a Crow tribe of Indians that once lived close by. They used this stone cliff to sharpen their spears for battle. Through the shear raking of the stone tips of their spears on this sandstone wall, they would grind them to a razor-sharp edge. The grinding of their spearheads speaks to me; it reminds me that as I work in community, prayer is the sole weapon of my faith. When was the last time we fought in prayer for the life of someone outside the family of God? It's not ours to strategize, but it is ours to take time each and every day to put an edge on one of the only weapons of our faith. Pray. Don't just grind on it. Hone it and polish it like the fine instrument it's meant to be, our very lifeline. Prayer is the discipline of a true warrior; it's a partnership with heaven. It cannot be solicited, nor can sheer determination suffice to get it done. God simply wants our availability. Neither the disciples nor Esther knew what lay in their future. And you and I, for that matter, really do not know what is over the next horizon. Warriors are everyday stuff. They set a watch every day and in the night.

7

ANDRIZOU

Christianity is greatest when it is hated by the world.
—St. Ignatius

As a youth and even in my early twenties growing up in the northwest, everyone seemed to somewhat agree as to how life was expected to be played out. *Multicultural* was a term that didn't even exist as far as I knew. The neighborhood differences were Protestant versus Catholic or Republican versus Democrat. There were little to no white/black issues because there were so few African Americans where we lived. Likewise, although they were more integrated in our communities, there was just a sprinkling of Mexicans. The Native Americans seemed to stay completely out of sight, and Asian people were unheard of completely. Obviously we are talking about a time and place that was predominantly white and middle class. It's positively amazing to contemplate the idea of rubbing close and interacting with a society that pretty much agrees with everything that you hold to be of value. Looking back at my life from a personal perspective in comparison to today's culture, it was shallow; there was no space for someone with a different color or background. Furthermore, there was a way you carried about your affairs that was considered normal, maybe casual, but for sure it fit the average person. Being a churchgoing person was still considered to be in that norm; however, letting it be known that you'd become a Christian began to narrow things down some, kind of like a person of color moving into an all-white neighborhood. I can still recall when this dividing line began to show up for me. Once it became known that I was a Christ follower, it was challenging. I found myself having to explain things to my former friends about my new friends and vice versa—until I realized I could no longer hide behind a false identity. I had to stand up to a new set of values. I had to *decide*, and things changed drastically!

Throughout the centuries and in various areas of the globe, there have been times and places where it has been more difficult than others to outwardly profess Christianity. Often, in other countries, such as Iran or Iraq, it's been essential to swear allegiance to a person or a belief system, thereby denying faith or loyalty to Jesus Christ, whereas in America, we've had our religious freedom. Not surprisingly, the winds of time are changing. For years already. the far eastern and western borders of our country have realized a constant influx of people who do not share the enthusiasm or the conviction of our Protestant denominations or the liturgical community of churches. It's no longer new or unique for them to make clear statements as to their beliefs, while challenging us on our own turf. This is how it has been since the beginning of the church. To whom do we swear our allegiance? We have to decide.

From the beginning of time, God has called a people who would be faithful to him at whatever the cost. This doesn't happen the same day we purpose in our hearts to follow Christ; however, the promise of God's abiding presence and his willingness to take us from where we are and develop us into people capable of representing him in the most dire of situations is in place. You will remember the apostle Paul's mention of this to his friends at Philippi; "being confident of this," he said, "that he who began a good work in you will carry it on to completion until the day of Jesus Christ" (Philippians 1:6 NIV). As far back as I can recall, in my pilgrimage, the unction for me has been to move forward in my Christian experience and watch as God works to prove himself in and around myself in whatever the situation. This is powerful! It's because of having lived these experiences that I hope to always give myself to stand up and decide for Christ, even in difficult times.

Joshua, a true warrior of early Bible times, had proven faithfulness and trust, thereby earning the right for Moses to hand him the baton of leadership over the children of Israel. It was at the time of his appointment that the God of the Israelites gave him a word that was intended to fortify him, to bolster him mentally, physically, and spiritually as he shouldered the rigors of this massive undertaking. Furthermore, he desires to give this word to each of us as we move forward against the tribulations of our own time. From the Hebrew language comes the title of this chapter, Andrizou (Joshua 1:7–9 NIV). Translated into English, Andrizou means to "be strong and courageous, act like a man," a powerful word for you and me as warriors of today. Many individuals who have sought God in situations that seemed impossible have heard heaven whisper, "Andrizou, be strong and act like a man." See the strength of the Lord! In my own experience, on one occasion in particular, I was desperate with God and had asked for a word in specific as to my next move, and it was as though it were audible, "Go straight forward." I knew it was God because it gave me courage, and it was an exercise in total trust. I didn't know any more than I had known earlier—except that now I was not alone.

Immediately following Christ's ascension into the glory of heaven, it became the responsibility of his disciples, along with the early church, to take the Gospel, the story of Jesus, throughout the then known world. You would agree after reading the four Gospels along with the book of Acts that there was sufficient energy to carry out the activity of what has come to be known as the Great Commission. However, now it became the responsibility of this handful of followers to not only tell the world around them but to energize them with that same power. What would this look like in the centuries to come? Throughout history, although critical situations have never been duplicated exactly, God most often uses an imperfect man (not gender specific) to lead even nations of people. A great example during that time in history was a man named Polycarp, who had earlier been a friend of John the apostle. Polycarp became one of those instrumental in transitioning the early church from the apostolic age into the second century. Fact is Polycarp was a second-century bishop of the church at Smyrna. In his time, the Roman state ruled; there was no compromise, and you had to swear allegiance to Lord Caesar. Notwithstanding, after many years of teaching his constituents to stand up for Christ and not Caesar, Polycarp was eventually confronted by the authorities but to no avail. For a short time, Polycarp fled and went into hiding. However, he was soon to give himself up to his capturers, who in turn delivered him to the proconsul, where he was to stand trial. Herod, the police captain, tried to persuade him, saying, "Why, what harm is there in saying 'Caesar is Lord,' and offering incense and thereby saving yourself." When they persisted, Polycarp responded by saying, "I am not about to do what you are suggesting to me." With further threats then, they rushed him into the stadium, where he was to face his martyrdom, "and as he was led to the stadium, there was such a tumult in the stadium that no one could even be heard."

"But as Polycarp entered the stadium, there came a voice from heaven, Andrizou, be strong, Polycarp, and act like a man. And no one saw the speaker, but those of our people who were present heard the voice." After further verbal torment and threats, Polycarp replied, "For eighty-six years I've been his servant and he has done me no wrong. How can I blaspheme my King who saved me." So finally, after threatening him with being thrown to the lions, the proconsul said to him, "I will have you consumed by fire, to which Polycarp replied: You threaten with fire that burns only briefly and after just a little while is extinguished, for you are ignorant of the fire of the coming judgment and eternal punishment, which is reserved for the ungodly. But why do you delay? Come, do what you wish."

When the results of the proconsul's interrogation were announced to the crowd in the stadium, they shouted in unison that Polycarp should be burned at the stake, and immediately they ran through the streets, gathering sticks and wood for the fire. While Polycarp offered up a prayer of thanksgiving to the Father for counting him worthy to be sacrificed in this fashion, the proconsul had him tied, the wood was stacked all around him, and the flame was then attached to what they hoped would become a human torch.

> "And as the mighty flame blazed up, we saw a miracle (we, that is, to whom it was given to see), and we have been preserved in order that we might tell the rest what happened. For the fire, taking the shape of an arch, like the sail of a ship filled with the wind, completely surrounded the martyr; and it was there in the middle, not like flesh burning but like bread baking or like gold and silver being refined in a furnace. For we also perceived a fragrant odor, as if it were the scent of incense or some other precious spice.

"When the lawless men eventually realized that this body could not be consumed by the fire, they ordered an executioner to go up to him and stab him with a dagger. And when he did this, there came out a large quantity of blood, so that it extinguished the fire; the whole crowd was amazed that there should be so great a difference between the unbelievers and the elect. Among them most certainly was this man, the most remarkable Polycarp, who proved to be an apostle and prophetic teacher in our time, bishop of the holy church in Smyrna." (Michael W. Holmes, *The Apostolic Fathers*, 2nd edition, pp. 135–144).

This truly is an amazing account, one of a man who was quite simply just a man. As his life began, he was no different from Joshua, Caleb, Esther, Nehemiah, Daniel, or any number of biblical characters after whom he chose to model. All of whom, for that matter, began their journey by at one time or another deciding to stand up and be counted among the people of God. Along their pilgrimage, they each made continual choices to firm up this commitment, and gradually they would be placed in difficult and stretching circumstances. One by one, the answer to their facing dilemma would prove their growing faith, until at a particular time in history or in the unfolding of an event, they were asked to step to the podium. At that particular point of contact, one where time and space seem to stand still, the whole world, as it would seem, watches as God makes his statement. The secular community among us, sad as it may be, fails to understand. In Polycarp's time, the stadium was in shock, and for that matter, history records the hard truth that persecution and martyrdom went on hold after Polycarp. The Roman world was forced to reconsider Christianity—the power and presence of believers, their aroma, their courage and stamina. Make no mistake we are salt and light to a dying world, and as such, we must make a difference. This is the only reason we exist.

A question deserving a spotlight remains to be, how did Polycarp, or anyone of us for that matter, get from a simple follower of Christ to being an exemplary model and eventually a martyr? That question begs a further question of us all regarding our total existence for Christ. Just briefly now, and only for the sake of a comparison, let me say that in a previous document I concluded that, "evangelism is not a shouting on the street corner or some knee jerk energy given to a non suspecting bystander, it's about recognizing opportunity and then turning opportunity into dialogue. Dialogue then exposes the Truth to which the lost world either embraces or rejects. But evangelism is not something we do for God, it is something that God does through us—it's Divine" (B. Stanley Tieszen, *Preacher and the Bear, Exploring Evangelisms Forgotten Frontier*). Similarly, being a martyr or finding ourselves in a situation of persecution isn't something we sign up for in specific; it's the result of an encounter with the living Christ and making an active decision to follow him. In today's Christian economy, we see people in some denominations who have raised their hands when an appeal is made for those who want to turn their backs on sin and be converted. In an instant, they are changed, but they will have to decide further; there will be a time when an act of volition becomes essential, literally turning their back on sin specifically, physically directing an effort in the opposite direction, thereby affirming that commitment. These and other gestures are acts of faith that energize us forever. Others from different church affiliations were baptized into the church, and as they grow to adulthood, some begin to question their position and rightly so. They along with the rest of us need an encounter with the Christ of the Bible. This is where the power resides; it's not in a list of do-good rules to somehow gain for us any self-righteousness. Salvation and power are found intellectually when we have become convinced in the living God. It is found emotionally when we have become convicted of our lost-ness to sin; we regret and remorse to the point of repentance. And finally, salvation is affirmed in an act of volition whereby our free will helps us to turn from sin to righteousness.

The word *volition* is not a common word in today's vocabulary, and it might be easier to remember when we use the word *intentional*. Looking at the conversion of the apostle Peter, we can easily see that he was quick to arrive intellectually at who Jesus was. Peter knew the scriptures well, and what Jesus was doing by healing the sick proved to Peter's mind of Jesus's identity. However, answering Jesus's question in Mark 8: 29 (NIV), "But what about you," he asked, "who do you say that I am?" Peter answered, "You are the Christ." In today's world, that would make him a believer. And rightly so, but Christianity is continually on the move. What this did for Peter was to give Jesus the right to take him from this early stage of believing to maturity. For Peter, this was a painful process because it required total transparency. It exposed the rough edges of his character—impulsiveness, dishonesty, and likely other traits that all defined a shallow Christlikeness. Then, of course, after all of the disappointments and embarrassments, we come to meet the new Peter, humbled and yet dedicated totally to Christ and his greater work. Had this process not occurred, Jesus would never have asked him later to "feed my sheep," a statement that in itself was a commissioning and eventually led to his own martyrdom. We, as well as Peter, have a free will that can take steps away from or toward the God who calls us.

I well remember myself as a young man, asking Jesus to forgive me of my sin so many times, and yet I would continue on in the same unchecked direction. Then a pastor friend once told me, "Bill, I don't think you have ever known Jesus." That day, I again invited Christ into my life. Something was different. I had always believed in God, but now I was crushed under the weight of my own sin. Now this represented my whole heart's attitude. It was a real encounter with Jesus. The next morning, I could hardly wait to examine my entire existence and carefully remove anything and everything that cluttered my life with counterproductive trinkets and literature. This was an act of volitional faith, and it affirmed my commitment to Christ. It was a life-changing event. It was intentional. What's more is that these lessons haven't stopped. Likewise, Polycarp's experience was that for eighty-six years in his service, there had grown such a trust that this would be a poor time to deny him. But we don't have a choice as to how we might one day represent the Christ that we serve. Will we be asked to stand in a jury to decide for a crime so justice will be served? Will we be a witness to a crime that we could easily hide away? Each of us will be asked differently to represent Christ. However, there are those who will never recognize a request to stand up for the one who saved them; the lack of total transparency and the indecision will keep them from the growth process of others. They will be lukewarm—no vibrancy, no witness, no power, and, consequently, no fruit bearing .

As we examine the story of Polycarp further, one could easily place too much energy on the pinnacle of his career, his martyrdom. This man's entire life, no different from yours or mine, was given to the work of the kingdom. He, like us, lived in some of the most difficult of times. Our own country has not been as divided as it is now for the past one hundred and fifty years, and it's making our lives an everyday challenge. Polycarp lived and ministered in near total disagreement with the law of his time. He disagreed with slavery, prostitution, murder, greed, and most of all, he disagreed with the politics of his time. We as Christians face these and other obstacles as well. In the history of mankind, has this ever been any different? The challenges of this day are found in the encroachment of a Godless society—secularism, freedom of choice versus pro-life, active homosexuality, gender choice and gender change, just to name a few. As the spotlight looks to examine the life of this martyr, it could easily become a beacon that lights the way for us and asks of us each a willingness to move forward. How will we decide? At what point do we engage, and to what are we challenged?

Jack Phillips, the owner of a cake shop in Colorado, denied his artistic cake decorating services to an openly gay couple wishing to be married. His decision was based on his religious beliefs. Jack claimed that his decorating skills would be compromised if he performed them for those who openly violated his biblically based belief, the principles of his faith. The cost for this decision, not to mention the stress, was enormous. Immediately, he faced losing his store and his livelihood. What was being expected of Jack, similar to Polycarp, was this question; why couldn't he agree to decorate a wedding cake, to spread a little frosting for a homosexual couple? It would be so simple. But Christians decide early on to whom they will devote their allegiance. While I don't know Jack personally, it's a good bet that this wasn't the first time he was asked to compromise; he had decided early on. The challenge for him was similar to that of Polycarp; it can no longer be satisfied by persuasive rhetoric. This is where the rubber meets the road. Your total existence is on the line. You have to decide.

In both of the above illustrations, Christian men were living in a society where compromise had gradually changed much of its citizenship to secularism. Slowly they became surrounded by circumstances that were out of their control, and contrary to the pressures of their time, both men continued to live according to the standard of conviction they had previously adopted. Then all of a sudden, they were challenged, and without compromise, the focus of each encounter was spent on the conquest of their mission, which was to stand up and represent the principles of their belief system. This is so similar to a military strategy. Of course you would want to return from a bombing exercise, but the mission, the real reason you would enlist, is to represent the person or the objective, regardless of the cost. All else has no spine.

Continuing under the spotlight of Polycarp's legacy reminds me of yet another aspect of persecution and martyrdom. Similar to Andrizou, the word of encouragement given to Polycarp at the onset of his experience, there is a biblical promise that augments our defense in times of direst. The apostle Mark records Jesus's words during the Olivetti discourse of Mark 13:1–17 (v. 11, NIV), "Whenever you are arrested and brought to trial, do not worry beforehand about what to say. Just say whatever is given you at the time, for it is not you speaking but the Holy Spirit." There was a time when illegal activity was taking place in our neighborhood. Because of the closeness of our residence to this ongoing crime activity, the county sheriff swore me in as an undercover deputy. I wore a concealed weapon and was made aware of more details than I wanted to know. The night that arrests were made, I was to stand guard at a home that had been used to store guns, some illegal, and grow marijuana. In addition, these same people managed some nearby ranch property that adjoined a creek bottom where numerous (many) marijuana gardens had been planted. These gardens were hand watered daily and developed a plant size of eight to nine feet in height. Because of the overall retail cost of this drug seizure, not to mention eventually crossing state lines, it ended as a nationally celebrated drug crime. Eventually, it became published in national newspapers as well as the nation's number one porn magazine. (Similar to the days of prohibition, the growth and sales of marijuana in many places is no longer illegal).

It wasn't long following the arrests that my name showed up as a witness to this crime. The accused, along with their attorneys, visited my job site to inform me of a subpoena that would be issued on my behalf, and I was terrified. Over time, the legal process developed, and true to their word, I was asked to take the stand. Without legal advice or counsel of any nature, I swore to tell the truth, so help me God. Within the next forty-five minutes to an hour, I was badgered by this bunch of thugs, and to my amazement, the answers I gave were completely out of my mind. With the testimony I gave that day, the defendants were put to shame. The truth was proclaimed in a court of law that could not be rebutted. After it had gone on for some time, the defense attorneys appealed to the judge for me to be stopped. The judge in turn reminded them that they had made a mockery of the legal system, and it was about time for the same treatment to be returned. The judge then turned to me with an approving smile and said, "Just answer the questions as they are asked." For years afterward, I encountered lawmen who wanted to shake my hand to show their gratitude for what happened that day. God was my defense, and he defended the laws of our land that are in place to protect the citizenship. We must remember this bit of scripture that wants to come to our defense and place it carefully in the file of our mind. It's not just an old history; it's a hidden principle of scripture meant to be employed by a servant and warrior at an appointed time.

When I read the accounts of Bible characters, I become energized. And to bring the energy of the apostolic age into the second century, it again took the example of someone God was able to trust to do that great work; it was a divinely infused energy. We must recognize within our spirit that this great energy is available, infectious, and contagious. It makes us want to be part of God's trusted few who can change the world around us. It's been said that people don't follow leaders; they follow courage.

During the time of Margret Thatcher's leadership in the UK, she made some difficult decisions that required her to dispatch a number of men from her cabinet. When confronted by Her Majesty, the queen, she said that her father had always told her, "God needs no faint hearts for his ambassadors." When asked to give an account for her actions, she said that her termination of these individuals "wasn't just their age that decided, their background mostly and lack of grit as a consequence of their privilege and entitlement." The queen then inquired if she was comfortable with having enemies, to which Margret responded, in the words of Charles Mackey:

> "You have no enemies, you say?
> Alas my friend, the boast is poor;
> He who has mingled in the frey
> Of duty, that the brave endure,
> Must have made foes! If you have none,

Small is the work that you have done.
You've hit no traitor on the hip, you've dashed no cup
from purge-ed lip.
You've never turned the wrong to right, you've been a
coward in the fight."
(Charles Moore, *Margret Thatcher, the Authorized
Biography: Herself Alone*, p. 729)

Let me be clear. It is the responsibility of each and every Christ follower to love their enemies and to live in harmony with those in society, regardless of their beliefs or sexual preferences. We are to live quietly and responsibly while making the most of opportunity in representing the living Christ to the world. Discipline will count just as much as courage. We have to decide!

8

WEAPONS, WATCHMAN, AND THE WARRIOR

Better a patient man than a warrior, a man who
controls his temper than one who takes a city.
—Proverbs 16:32 (NIV)

Weapons—Provision and Position, Posture and Purpose

From the book of Ephesians, the apostle Paul gives the church a clear and comprehensive description of the weaponry against our adversary, the devil and his cohorts. As it comes to us, the letter to the Ephesian people may likely have been intended for the Laodicean church. Scofield says (the introductory to Ephesians) that it may not have been sent to the church of Ephesus in particular, but it may have been carried to several churches, thereby making it a letter to the church at large. My mind immediately wants to go to the sixth chapter and study what's considered to be the Christian's arsenal for warfare; however, it's essential to use the entire book so as to keep things in context as well as allow scripture to influence the whole person. This is what seems to be intended. As is common for Paul, he begins his letter as a prayer; he thanks God wholeheartedly for those who have come to follow Christ, those whom God has chosen before the foundation of the world. However, his ambition for them is not to go out and fight the devil. It's Paul's wish that God would "give you a spirit of wisdom and revelation, that you would know him better" (Ephesians 1:17 NIV). He's not as interested in these parishioners becoming fighters as he is in them growing up in Christ. As it pertains to the adversary, we as humans want to either step to the side and avoid any conflict or we want to put up our fists. At this point, we must see the striking contrast between the way the world views the warrior and the intention Christ has for his church. Paul is not talking about a lone vigilante with a sharpened spear intent on doing physical harm. His first thought is that we should be enlightened (1:16). He's getting to the power idea that we are so interested in but that will be the result of this enlightenment—to be free from ignorance and misinformation. What's being said is that we begin to prepare for battle as we appropriate our standing with Christ, to literally take hold of the *provision* of Christ.

Paul asks us two times in the first paragraph of the second chapter to "remember" who we once were, but "now in Christ Jesus you who once were far away have been brought near through the blood of Christ." Paul will eventually get to the idea of putting on the full armor of Christ, but first he wants to prepare us for the journey. What's our responsibility? To begin with, we must appropriate this divine provision, the blood of Christ shed for us, thereby establishing our position. Once we understand this and apply it, the power is there for us. In a literal sense, we as Christians aren't going hunting, spiritual warfare is a battle fought through our personal preparation and prayer. This poopoos the idea of raising your hand, and instantly you become a warrior for Jesus. Rightfully taking our position reminds the devil that what he wants to steal from us, what he wants to kill in us, and what he longs to destroy in us is not his to have. He is defeated from the onset, but you will be challenged!

Following weekend services recently, I was approached by a man I have known, if only slightly, for many years. We greeted each other, and he immediately began to inform me of a situation with his wife that was upsetting. Apparently, through some misbehavior on his own part, he had given reason for his wife not to trust him, and although he had asked for forgiveness for what he had done, she was unwilling to oblige him. Now she badgered this man continually. It became immediately clear to me that this couple needed counseling; however, I sensed as well that the unwillingness of her to forgive set up the possibility of a stronghold, a wall of resistance that the enemy of our soul uses as a foothold. I realized that this man's poor decision to violate their marriage vows gave another opening to the enemy. While we both knew it was a sin on his part that brought this division, I suggested that he begin to pray against this barrier, to remind the devil that they both belonged to Christ, that their marriage vows were sealed in heaven, and that he is a defeated foe. The final intentions for the enemy, here of course, are to destroy their lives as husband and wife. True healing will take time because a trust has been broken, but as we pray, God will level the playing field. Then he begins to soften hearts, he gives wisdom to our actions, and, most of all, he sends the enemy packing. Note: you can bet that God will impress on this man the severity of his foolishness. He understands at this point that he sinned all right, but he qualifies it as a one in his private scale of one to ten on sin, which, generally speaking, is based on his own misinformation. One could say that the core of his deficiency lies in a total ignorance of Holy Writ. Sin is sin, and you never give ground to the devil, as you have no idea the grave depths of the consequences. This is where we begin to learn and experience God's power, but we cannot sit idly by. Yes, a grave mistake has been made, but so often, this is the only way we can learn.

Notice the unattractive parallel here from Ephesians (NIV). Paul prays "that the eyes of our hearts be enlightened" (1:18), and my friend didn't have a clue at what I was saying. To be enlightened has a double meaning. First of all, it confirms the word *ignorance* presented in chapter 4:18, and second, it is meant to include misinformation. He has taught himself to live without the regular influence of scripture, while he has allowed our world's social system sufficient space to influence his behavior. For myself, I have committed this little quote to memory: "Love for truth is the cornerstone of spiritual life as well as an assurance of our spiritual survival when the society's conscience has joined forces with the world" (*The Orthodox Veneration of Mary the Birthgiver of God*). Through biblical illiteracy, my friend has become blinded by the god of this age. He's ignorant, misinformed, and he's not enjoying "the inheritance" (1:14) in the saints. This man is no different from the natives that he despises for not getting on with a civilized culture. He's still insisting on living on the dirt floor of his unkempt spiritual lodge, while his Father's inheritance, God's personal gift to him, lies in waste. And this is the case for many supposed Christian people; they have played church all their lives when Christianity is the intentional investment of our total selves. Make no mistake, spiritual poverty, more accurately biblical illiteracy, is a culture that must be broken. This is part of the battle. It's for our own souls, and it is only a determined and desperate individual who can break this cultural bondage. This is a stubbornness that begs for deliverance.

It's important to know that the many articles that scripture identifies as true weapons of our arsenal are not listed in specific here, and furthermore, scripture does not give them as a list per se. Each of these should become treasures discovered by us personally through our study and devoted pilgrimage. One afternoon while visiting with a friend, he openly shared that he had become totally enlightened by a discovery. He said in his excitement, "Did you know that kindness is a weapon against the devil?" Well, no, I hadn't recognized it as such, at least until he opened it up to me. I do know that the discovery for him was as powerful as the word itself. This discovery came by way of divine revelation brought on by study and a life fully engaged in pilgrimage. (Check out the fruit of the Spirit, Galatians 5:22 [NIV] to see if in fact they all are not weapons against the devil.) Had he simply read a list of supposed weaponry, it would have failed him in the time of his greatest need, but his was a discovery at an appointed time, specific to a current need. This is the wisdom and revelation of verse 1:17 that we spoke of earlier. The Catholic Church believes quite strongly that praying the rosary is a vital weapon against the adversary, and rightfully so. If this were something to be challenged as a Protestant, don't take it up with your Protestant friends; there's much information by biblical scholars that will help you to better understand. As a former Protestant, this has become a discovery on my own part. The purpose here, however, is not to make a Protestant become a Catholic or vice versa; it is for us to discover for ourselves just who and what are our helpers, the real weapons in our battle against the devil. And there are many. This is not superstition; it's supernatural!

Posture and Purpose

Posture, as defined by *Webster's*, is "an upright position to prevent backache." Those with whom I have regular contact already know from our past dealings what my conversation will sound like. They know my stand on pornography, the vocabulary I've chosen, and many other social issues. Not long ago, a business acquaintance told me a story that was very funny, but I became disappointed that I had even heard it. The next time I had occasion to see him, he intended to take it up from where he left off, and I was forced to tell him that I had a difficult time scrubbing his last story from my mind. I'll confess that some of these weak characteristics of our former way of life take a long time to bring into alignment, but now my friend knows where I stand. Without any further embarrassment, he knows my posture. All of this is for but one purpose—to be a warrior, a true soldier of the cross. These are disciplines that not only make us strong for the time of battle; they are what is expected of us. It's a holiness of God. Through each of the first five chapters of Ephesians, Paul continues to give instruction for Christian living. Quite simply, we cannot engage in combat with any real display of godly power or lasting consequence without this lifestyle. As we shall see in the identity of a warrior, this is a spiritual fight, one that is an extension of our very lives.

Watchman

The Crow Indians used to call them their wolves, the watchdogs of the entire encampment. Without several wolves in place throughout the day and night, the village would not be safe. An enemy tribe might likely be seeking revenge from the loss of a family member in a recent battle, or they might want to steal horses. Nonetheless, these wolves were an indispensable lifeline. Although to us in modern civilization, this might seem a bit barbaric, it's a biblical concept as well, ever since early biblical time. At one point, God told Ezekiel, for example, "Son of man I have made you a watchman for the house of Israel; so hear the word I speak and give them warning from me. When I say to a wicked man, You will surely die, and you do not warn him or speak out to dissuade him from his evil ways in order to save his life, that wicked man will die for his sin and I will hold you accountable for his blood. But if you do warn the wicked man and he does not turn from his wickedness or from his evil ways, he will die for his sin, but you will have saved yourself" (Ezekiel 3:18–20 NIV).

We've all heard numerous renditions of what in today's Christian culture might be termed as *accountability*. In our modern times, we understand the value of maintaining a good body life in our affairs of church, and we see as well that church attendance on a regular basis can help to achieve that purpose. However, those who fail in this minimal exercise of family gathering will most generally fail in any close, sustainable relationships outside of a church gathering as well. During one particular men's group fellowship I attended, the speaker made an attempt to have each man at our table of six be accountable to one another. I'm sorry, but this was not going to work that way at all; it was a pipe dream. What I mean is that unless and until we've found someone with whom we can both share ourselves and hear from them on the everyday stuff of life, we simply won't find accountability. To begin with, in the bigger picture, we must be accountable to the local church. It's family. Here there is safety. But I promise you that each person is in need of one or two others with whom they can be perfectly candid. Not only will this take place aside from the normal church setting, but it will require time to fully develop. Anyone can see that this type of dependence is going away in modern society because of the busyness of our schedules and the independence of today's lifestyle. However, it is a necessity for wholesome Christian living. It's not just that we share our lives with each other; we remember each other to the Father, allowing this to become more than a casual, spur-of-the-moment kind of thing. We hear complications with work or family, and it's not as though we give advice; we are there to listen and be of support. We pray continually for one another, which gives us a strength of character. This is where iron sharpens iron and, like the natives of long ago, we become the watchdogs. It's an indispensable lifeline.

We should feel strong enough about this type of wholesome body life that we explore it further. Fact is I believe that God cares about this particular need, and he should be central to the discovery of such a person or persons in our lives. I would never sit back and brainstorm the thought of just who could or would fill this need for me. I would take it directly to the immediate attention of the Father. This will take time, but after speaking candidly with heaven, just decide to be a casual observer for a time. This is no different from anything I ever do regarding spiritual concerns; it's supernatural. Watch as God seems to place people in your life and circumstance. Possibly through normal conversation you begin to suspect a uniqueness about an individual, and you begin to ask yourself if there is something going on here. Taking it to the next level is anyone's guess; however, at this time, you will want to know if this person can be serious. Can they be confidential? Are there some similarities between you, and are they interested in visiting again? Court this relationship to where you can feel comfortable and the feeling becomes mutual. What might happen if you were to introduce a prayer together or maybe offer to pray about something that came up as a need for this individual? This in itself should be gratifying. Make it short and sweet, and then watch as each individual will long for this to grow. It's really not essential to introduce the spouses and go bowling. This is a very special person or persons. One day, through normal conversation, this person (either of you, for that matter) might ask a sensitive question, and it could be that they hadn't even intended to. Will the two, or three, of you be able to bare your souls and through humility build each other up? This sort of thing has happened to me, and I will say that it's positively one of the most exciting times I have in my life. My wife will tell you that this has proven to be a positive lifeline for me. These are my friends. We guard each other without making an announcement about it. We pray together and for each other privately. We are so unlike one another, and yet we have found that our particular needs are so similar. I will say that when this can work, you will begin to see that you just do not want to be without them. Others are meant to complete us! Independence, on the other hand, stands at the door of carnality, whereas together we are growing to become true warriors. Needless to say, I want this more than anything in my world because it stands in full support of my wife and family, church and ministry, work and outreach, and consequently the safety of the entire village community of my life.

Warriors

Searching the scriptures on the subject title of a warrior provokes yet further thought. Who were some biblical warriors? What did the activity of warring actually accomplish, and was this activity carried on past the captivity of the children of Israel by the Babylonians or the Assyrians? In other words, can we assume that the battles we face today are to be fought without bloodshed? As you may recall from the lessons of Ezekiel, God alone was their defense at that point, and the only weapons they were to use were "prayer, obedience and trust." Furthermore, the New

Testament fails to record any battle such as was told when David fought and killed Goliath or when the walls of Jericho were demolished and its inhabitants annihilated. Nonetheless, the first actual record of a warrior is from a song that the children of Israel sang after they had been rescued from the pursuing Egyptian army as they were drowned in the middle of the Red Sea. Jehovah God rescued them, and they assigned him the title, "The Lord is a warrior, the Lord is his name" (Exodus 10:3 NIV). From that early point and on through to the conquering of the land of their inheritance, we find that God's ambition about combat was to use the Israelites, his chosen people, to literally rub out the Godless nations that inhabited the land. There were many battles that the children of Israel fought as they pushed forward to this final conquest, and the bloodshed of both man and beast ran deep. However, from my earlier studies in a survey of the Old Testament, the lasting impression was not that God was an ocher or a bloodthirsty king, as some would like to believe; he had an everlasting love for his people but a vengeful hate for sin. He hated idolatry and pagan worship, which was physically torturous, sexually promiscuous, and murderous to the sacrificing of human beings—killing babies and throwing them to the flames of a furnace. In today's economy, the sins of society are no less promiscuous; however, nowhere in the scriptures are we invited to engage in any way other than "pray, obey and trust." Each of us must stay true to our convictions and what the legal system will allow us to do, while being at the total mercy of God himself. And then, without compromise, we stand our ground.

Going back to our study, we've looked closely at all but the last view verses of the book of Ephesians, and at this point, we desperately want to know why Paul begins chapter 6 verse 10 by saying, "Finally." However, if we apply these next ten verses and eliminate the first five plus chapters, we will be defeated in the entire mission. "Finally" is intended only as Paul's last bit of helpful advice. It's a crescendo, so to speak, and highly valuable but of no more importance than the entire book as you fight the good fight of faith. To be the warrior that God has intended us to be requires our focused attention on Christlikeness. The definition of the armor of God and the identity of Satan's war machine, his hierarchy, is information meant to be the study of a lifetime and is found throughout the scriptures. It's a never-ending list of information that tends to stimulate our thinking, but information gets stored away, and we are left to wonder rather than be challenged. There is much more to this, however; it will only be found and learned during our daily walk and upon each person's individual experience or encounter. A more scholarly view may be necessary, or the counsel of a seasoned exorcist could be sought out, however, similar to the apostle Peter when he was asked if he believed and he said, "Lord I believe, help my unbelief," and the Lord did exactly that. So we say with heartfelt desire and conviction, "Please, Lord, teach me." And it's with this attitude of mind that God wants to give his instruction, one that will be lasting and will go with us into the battle. A true warrior then will be a student of Christian living who exercises the principles of scripture. They give themselves continually to a walk of uprightness and sensitivity to the Holy Spirit's guidance. This person may not be the one who stands out in the crowd but will be the person with whom others care to listen.

While Jeremiah was a prophet of the Lord, he was a true warrior as well. His messages were daring, to say the least, but they were always preceded with "This is what the Lord says." By experience, he had learned that not only did he have nothing to say personally, but that prayer and a Word from the Lord were the only weapons of his faith. For Jeremiah, a Word from the Lord is for us today the Word of the Lord, and it is a formidable weapon against our wicked opponent, the devil. Jeremiah could recall, by reading the Pentateuch, when the children of Israel left Egypt. He could visualize Pharaoh, now regretting that he had freed those he used as slaves, riding after them with horses and chariots. He could recall times of persecution in his own life when he was falsely accused of the delivery of punishing prophetic utterances, foretelling catastrophic events that his superiors strongly objected to. He could look back now at the closing of his book and remember the many times his life was in danger and his only defense was the weapons of his faith. He is reminded of all of this in his closing prayer to the Lord: "You are my war club, my weapon for battle—with you I shatter nations, with you I destroy kingdoms, with you I shatter horse and rider, with you I shatter chariot and driver, with you I shatter man and woman, with you I shatter old man and youth, with you I shatter young man and maiden, with you I shatter shepherd and flock, with you I shatter farmer and oxen, with you I shatter governors and officials" (Jeremiah 51:20, 23 NIV). It becomes obvious that each of these individuals or circumstances had at one time been an adversary to Jeremiah. He never tortured or killed anyone. He was not known to be a threat of any kind, but he was known for his obedience to God, his commitment to the Word of the Lord and in personal prayer. Jeremiah was a man of impeccable faith, a student and prayer warrior to be emulated.

9

LOSING OUR EDGE

Achan replied, "It is true ! I have sinned
against the Lord, the God of Israel."
—Joshua 7:20, 22 (NIV)

Most would agree that the many events recorded in the pages of the Bible
have become the stories we so frequently tell. Some are the accounts of
common people, and others are of kings and kingdoms. To say only that
they are historic would be an understatement; they have effectively touched
the very hearts of men, women, and children down through the centuries.
We love to tell the story of David being the youngest member of his family
and assigned the lowly task of a shepherd boy. Then one day while delivering
some food supplies to his brothers on the battlefront, he confronts the
greatest challenge of his adolescent life—Goliath, the giant of the enemy
forces of the Philistines! After miraculously slaying this belligerent brute
with a small, smooth stone launched from his slingshot, David's fame
takes him from one harrowing experience to another, and eventually he
wins the throne. David becomes king of the land! And then there is the
heartwarming story of Mary, the birth giver of the Son of God. The pages
of the Bible literally come alive when the angel Gabriel appears to tell her
that she is highly favored and would be overshadowed by the Almighty
to conceive and bear a Son, and not just any son but the long awaited
Savior and ruler of the world. Mary's humble response of submission and
obedience are reflected in the few words spoken spontaneously from the
willingness of her tender heart, "May it be to me as you have said" (Luke

1:18b NIV). Those few words will forever penetrate the heart of reader and listener alike. And likewise, biblical history makes a record of those to whom we might look at with contempt because of misbehavior or a poor decision. So from the most humble and submissive to the calloused and hardened alike, these people, surrounded as it were by their events, become more than bedtime stories or historical accounts; they define the stuff of life itself from history past. Woven into these stories are some of the most profound principles of Christian living, and it's upon these principles that our faith and lifestyles find their rest.

Along with the heroic stories are accounts where disobedience has played its hand, and with no apology, the scriptures tell of their grievous ending. And just as you might imagine, this is the tragic introduction to an even more tragic story, the short story of Achan. The scriptures always tell it like it is; not once is there record of an account that glamorizes or smooths over the sin of an individual or a nation. God made it plain from the very beginning of time that sin in mankind would not go unpunished (or unpublished, as the case may be). Not only so, but the sins recorded from the scriptures also reflect their far-reaching effect; sin will follow a generational line. It will affect a family, a people, a business, or a nation. And such is the case of the man Achan. When the children of Israel, now under the leadership of Joshua, went in to lay claim to the land of their promise, God gave them specific instructions for each encounter, like an ongoing reminder of their dependence upon him. He wanted them to know that it wasn't by their prowess as warriors or in a specific battle strategy that they would be the victors, but only in their absolute obedience to his commands. The battle at Jericho was one of those signature situations where, by simply following his explicit instructions, however peculiar they might be, the walls of that great city would crumble to the ground—and they did. The battle against Jericho was the first triumphal engagement as they pressed in to lay claim to their new land.

It's after the tremendous victory at Jericho that the children of Israel seemingly become more confident and begin to strategize how the city of Ai might be conquered as well. Previously, all of God's people were involved in the battle of Jericho. Only now on this occasion, after spying out the city, Joshua makes the announcement that just two or three thousand men would be needed for this encounter. Long story short, the children of

Israel were the ones defeated; they were run off, and the lives of more than thirty warriors were lost. Immediately after receiving news of these losses, Joshua became grief stricken, and during his lament, God began a stern conversation with Joshua, alerting him of a sin that brought about these troubling consequences. It had been part of their instruction in the previous battle that Israel was told specifically not to take any of the plunder from that city; they were only to destroy it completely—men, women, children, livestock, and real estate. However, during the encounter, our man Achan discovered a much-coveted Babylonian garment and several bars of silver that seemed to call to him, and it was this unsavory attraction that led him to disobey God's instruction. And now somehow the confidence that had proven sufficient for the children of Israel's first military encounter was missing; they were routed by this seemingly smaller city, and they literally ran from these opposing forces. The children of Israel had lost their strength. The reputation that had preceded them ever since crossing the Jordan was gone. The joyous singing and celebration of the defeat at Jericho had vanished from sight, and God's chosen had lost their edge!

To draw an exact parallel between the lessons of the children of Israel in the Old Testament and the Christian community of today would seem unfair; however, one should look intently throughout the scriptures to garner, so to speak, these somewhat hidden principles that God tried to establish in his people from the beginning of time. The methods of their engagement in battle always differed one from another, but the principles stayed the same. For example, earlier, God had instructed Moses that it was his intention that there be a "distinction" between the children of Israel (in our time, the Christian community) and the people of this world, a principle that spoke directly to their everyday behavior (Exodus 33:15–16 NIV). And now very specifically through the actions of Achan comes another principle: there will be consequences for disobedience. And in the case at mention, these consequences will prove to be both personal and tribal. With this in mind, it has become startling to me how God continues to use his people of today as an influence in the world. We need to be honest with ourselves. If we go no further with this thought than a personal evaluation, I think it could have great value. Seriously, I don't think the Christian community looks that good to the world that we have been entrusted to influence. There is strong evidence to prove that the world is in an intense search for authenticity, and the hypocrisy of the so-called Christian community keeps them at bay. I wonder at my own actions at times. Could I have been kinder to a clerk at the counter? Did I show respect to our waitress? Does the way I drive cause some to detest me as a player in this supposed field of eternal offerings? We would agree that each of us could improve in these areas, as they are ongoing and we are the church, that living vibrant extension of heaven on earth. Now comes the question: how do we begin to apologize to the world?

I am convinced that if it is a single offense, then we make repairs on an individual basis. With a heart of honest repentance, we make our appeal to that specific individual. However, if the offense has been of a public nature, the correction must be commensurate. A great example for us today would be the archbishop of France who just recently, through a public announcement, said that the Catholic Church is aware of the accusations against some in the priesthood who have sexually molested young children. He also said that in the past, accusations of this nature had been handled within their own leadership; now he felt that in order to accomplish this more effectively, it needed to be given to a higher court of law for an unbiased investigation. While making this decision, he was forced to look at his own position carefully and weigh out the possible damage that this could incur to his own rank and reputation; what might be the cost to him personally? However, he also saw that this type of cleansing could be a powerful tool of evangelism for the greater church, and one would have to agree. People are more willing to follow courage than they are to follow leaders. This message would confirm to the world our undying belief in the principles of our faith. For others of us, regardless of the offense to an individual or to society, this may require some counsel, but we must be willing to take serious action. As the focus of the defeat at Ai was weighed out and the sin of Achan was brought to the forefront, the punishment he received was death and total destruction for the man himself as well as his entire family, his home, livestock, and all of his belongings.

This kind of punishment seems overly ambitious to us today. We simply cannot wrap our minds around it; however, in God's economy, this is how he looks at sin. Yes God is a God of kindness and love and mercy, but he is a God of justice. Justice identifies sin, its reward for omission and its punishment for committing. Personally, I want to curl up in a heap when

I even consider this in our world today. The prayer that I so often say for myself and my own community of family, neighbors, and church is "God have mercy, God have mercy!" I believe that he hears these prayers, but for us to say out of one side of our face that "Jesus is the same yesterday, today and forever" (Hebrews 13:8 NIV), we then have to believe that the church, which now stands figuratively as the children of Israel, is suffering from a continual state of being penalized; we've lost our edge. Our sins, the sins of the church and its people at large, the sins of the clergy, both Protestant and Catholic, in unapologetic, unpunished pedophilia, are punishing us today. The prophet Jeremiah said it like it is: "Your wickedness will punish you; your backsliding will rebuke you. Consider then and realize how evil and bitter it is for you when you forsake the Lord your God and have no awe of me" (Jeremiah 2:19 NIV). Could it be that our sins, both individual and corporate, are dampening the testimony of the greater church?

Looking at the lesson of Achan seems so antiquated, one could say, but as in so many other instances, these were the principles the children of Israel were to live by, and this punishment left an unforgettable impression. In today's Christian lifestyle, it's the norm to do things for the sake of our belief system because we too follow these same principles. We give to the church because it's a biblical principle. We even give to the poor because the scriptures tell us that they will always be a part of our communities, and they are not to be treated as refuse. Often we do these things to ease our conscience; however, most of us have learned that there is a reward for this obedience. This gift giving follows biblical principles; by faith, there will be a greater reward one day. But why does our conscience somehow stop at a point where we can no longer get past it emotionally or economically? Like the bishop of France, we must be willing to make a biblically based decision and let the chips fall where they may.

Frequently throughout my lifetime, there have been occasions when the Holy Spirit has brought conviction from the past that, although these offenses have been covered by repentance in my early Christian life, they now seem to reappear. It's like a serious personal reflection. If I was going to move forward in my Christian experience and expect any form of effective vibrancy in the community where I've been placed, I had to listen closely and follow my heart, as the tenderness of this vital organ that has been placed deep into my very soul had to be heard. There is always a positive effect to this character adjustment, but I can say with great assurance that had I not listened closely, my heart would have lost some of its sensitivity. This is about the still, small voice that calls out to us, and we must be attentive. "Above all else guard your heart because it is the wellspring of life" (Proverbs 4:23 NIV). I'm not suggesting that we become overly sensitive and crushed over the silly, minute trivia of life, but the Holy Spirit of God, being true to his character, must nudge us on occasion, encouraging us to do the right thing. Often, after hearing this prompting, we tuck the thought away, and then it comes back. Only now we acknowledge the voice but think no more of it—and it happens again and at a most unusual time. While there might only be minutes between these subtle contacts, it may be months or even years, but make no mistake, these nudges are divinely orchestrated and at appointed times. Life could and should follow a predictable path, a pattern that has been repeated from the beginning of time; it's a life of living for self and experiencing the lack of inner satisfaction. Adjustments are made, and we live in the reward of this new enlightenment. Things seem smooth, and then there's another interruption, another nudge like we mentioned previously. And try as we might, we avoid this at all costs. Long story short, this is how it works, and God knows when to expose these areas of our lives, and he knows how long it's going to take to truly get our attention, but make no mistake—God is 100 percent committed to our maturity as well as our fruit bearing.

I am reminded of a subject I have always been sensitive to, so much so that when I became engaged to be married to my wife, I knew this had to be addressed. And so when the time seemed right, I told her of an experience that I had immediately following my military discharge, where I had been accused of a girl's pregnancy. I was certain as to my innocence and told her so. It's without question that she needed my transparency; she needed to know of this incident. Quite honestly, typical of guy behavior, that was all that I was good for at that time in my life, and it seemed to cover the bases. But a couple of years later, I was reminded of it again and again, and I continued to hide under the idea of it not being my responsibility. Years later, there was another slight nudge and then another, until it became obvious that to satisfy my inner self, I needed a better answer. While it's not necessary to go into all of the details, an agency was hired to investigate, and they discovered that the child born to this girl, now grown of course, lived in the western states, just as I did, only many miles away. After contacting this individual through the agency, it was agreed to submit to DNA testing to either eliminate me or award me the fatherhood of this now grown child. Permission was agreed to and, long story short, the results came back as 99.99998 percent positive. I am the guy responsible. Roger became my part to pay in an apology to the world and to God for my actions that caused a grievous, statistical stress on our society.

There is much that could be said as to the emotions and actions of a young man as he grows up in a family not truly his own. Feelings of anger due to rejection and the not knowing of his rightful parenting caused Roger some years of severe pain, due to poor decisions on my part. I am pleased to say that our relationship, since this initial encounter, has become an ongoing process of growth together. One of the most gratifying things that has happened over the years of our acquaintance was when Roger sent me a text saying, "Bill, our discovery of each other has affected my path for the better. I have a completeness from it. The dim view of the unknown is past. I'm a man with a father who sought him. That's a ton of stuff man. I no longer feel different when discussing parents with friends. I can point at a picture and say this is my father and be eye to eye with others. And I feel I'm a part of this beautiful thing we call life. I always felt apart or left out. And the perpetual curiosity died out. I now know and I'm grateful. Not many could do what you have done. We good boss! Promise! No fading or lagging at all." And I must say that this has proven to be a tremendous joy for me. Occasionally now, as someone becomes privy to our situation, they have a look of curiosity. Some will stare into the distance, and I will know. For certain, there have been others who have been forced to review their own past and wonder.

Obviously, this isn't everyone's story, but that's not the point. And I'm not a hero for doing what I did, but I followed the cry of my heart. From this ongoing experience, there continues to be some interesting lessons. For one, it has become easy to see that faraway gaze of those who know that there is that black dot in their own vision. They may not be the parent of an illegitimate child, but there is something that seems to block their focus. This is a mark of the unknown. Although they do not know it at this time, it affects the vibrancy of their testimony, and their productivity as a part of the church in particular is ineffective. While the sins of the clergy have kept the greater church ruinlessly ill prepared for this solemn hour, the sins of individual parishioners fail to recognize that there is a tremendous battle that is raging, and we are to be a part of it. How and when we engage depends on our own authenticity. More than the use of military hardware, God asks our willingness to follow him. The cost is weighed out as we evaluate our real identity as a Christ follower. This is more than showing up to church for Sunday services, and it's past being a good neighbor. Following the Lord with all your heart unleashes the power of heaven into your circumstances like never before. It will affect the total of your circle of influence. It will bring repair to areas that you didn't know were damaged, and the shell of insecurity will begin to fade away.

A word of caution that I learned firsthand in this heartrending experience was that of my counsel. The seriousness of the illustration shown above convinced me to take this matter under strict confidential advice. I brought my convicting situation to three mature Christian friends, all professionals in ministry and counseling. With them, there was no encouragement at all to pursue this matter any further, and in fact, one of them said, "Don't kick a sleeping dog." This response infuriated me, as it shows a weakness, a chink in our armor one could say, of the supposed warriors of our Christian heritage. There eventually was a cost economically, not to mention the news to my immediate family. It was painful, but today it leaves me with no regret at all. The rewards have already proven to be tremendously gratifying, not to mention the applause of heaven one final day.

10

THE POWER

But you have planted wickedness, you have reaped evil,
You have eaten the fruit of deception.
Because you have depended on your own strength.
—Hosea 10:13 (NIV)

Architecture is a study that has always stirred a deep curiosity for me because, as it is said, architecture is a study in history. What's more is that if this is true of architecture, then more so the church. The church and Christianity are more than conversion, baptism, and going to heaven when you die; it's an examination of church history itself, not only from centuries past but yours as you observe, remember, and compare. This is demanding because it's beyond the reading of books. It will encompass all of life itself, and at times it will render you powerless. It's a mystery. Furthermore, as you seek an intimacy with our heavenly Father, you will find it, although it may frequently stretch you past your natural ability to endure. Often, the ambition and the initiative that one might exert on behalf of our faith, to stand up and be counted so to speak, will be denied as well, thereby adding yet another dimension to this total lack of comprehension. Adding again to the magnitude and the complexity of our faith is the element of surprise. Christianity and the church encompass many of the unpredictable circumstances of life. So when they occur, we must be willing to view these somewhat mysterious circumstances from a larger perspective. Many times, the things we cannot control are about change. It's an announcement of sorts.

As the experiences described above often place us in somewhat of a darkness of mind, we must be willing to move forward even with the miniscule amount of light that we have. This is not necessarily physical movement but a mental engagement of sorts acknowledging the moment. This is true faith, stepping forward when all you know is that quite possibly God wants you to act on his behalf. Most often, there will be sufficient time if only to whisper, "God have mercy." Please know that on occasion, you may feel like a blithering fool, but at the same time, God will not disappoint you, and in the end, you will not disappoint yourself. This will be a demonstration of the Spirit's work because this is where the power resides.

In retrospect, as I look at ministry opportunities that seemed to have flourished in my life, I've come to see that there was little that I did to initiate them as an event to pursue; they just happened. By a mistake or perhaps at the far side of a real-life struggle, they appeared to drop from the sky and to present themselves as opportunities to pursue, and the rest became history. One cannot help but notice here the peculiarity in what's just been said. On one hand, we push forward to prove our dedication in loving and serving Christ or in the pedigree that we have earned, and it's denied, while on the other hand, achievement seems to have been found solely by our obedience and willingness to follow. We do represent the church, however, and to recognize God in these unique situations should be our obligation. This is part and particular of our life's story. It's not just *comme ci, comme ca*. God is the potter, and we are the clay. We must be able to hear and see disappointments or change as a platform for opportunity and acknowledge them as such.

This is all optional of course. Not everyone is interested in having a positive approach to life's challenges. There are always those who have allowed talent and giftedness to lie dormant over the years, and they are not willing to move ahead under any circumstances. The Old Testament tells us of Joshua and Caleb, who welcomed the challenge of defeating the giants of the land, whereas there were those who turned a bitter cheek rather than embrace the trial as an obstacle to overcome (Numbers 13 and 14 NIV). The Bible has a tremendous amount to say about overcomers of difficult situations. When these things come against us, at some point in our existence, we should learn to be humbled before the Lord and ask for his sufficiency. He longs to be there for us. In the case of Joshua and Caleb, there was a severe penalty for the doubt that clouded the decision of the ten fearful spies of the children of Israel. They, along with all of the people who were twenty years of age and older, perished out on the desert plains before God asked them again to go in and possess the land of their inheritance. They had treated God with contempt (Numbers 14 and 15 NIV). Whenever God has a chore for us to do, it is never intended that we do it depending on our own strength or resources. Furthermore, this is a principle of scripture that holds true for each and every crisis that shows up to slap us around. God says it plain and simple, "In this world you will have trouble. But take heart! I have overcome the world" (John 16:33b NIV).

Power in Peculiar Circumstances

There was a time when I became invested in men's group fellowship. It all started out as a mistake when a friend asked me if I would lead a men's group breakfast. I agreed, and so we invited two other guys, and it was the four of us who would join hands in this supposed Christian setting where we were to learn and grow. You know, where iron sharpens iron, that sort of thing. Just like anything, there is a cost, a learning curve, in these situations. And according to plan, the guy with the great idea never showed up, and so we abandoned the thought. But it wasn't long until the same person asked me why we weren't meeting, and I simply told him the obvious reason—he never showed up. He asked if we could try this little project again. I agreed, and the same thing happened. This time, I sensed that something else was going on, so I continued with the group fellowship, only now I invited someone to replace my friend. This time, there was a new energy. However, while I was happy that men were showing up, I did all of the preparation, and it became exhausting. Out of desperation on one of our morning get-togethers, I simply took a scripture verse that had impressed me from my daily quiet time and wrote it on the back of a business card. The fact is I wrote out one for each of the guys. During our breakfast, I introduced the verse and gave each person a card. We read it together, talked briefly about it, and then I suggested that they *not* memorize the verse but put it in a convenient place and read it at least once a day. As I spoke, I shared with them how I discovered the verse and what it meant to me. Bingo! This was magic. These guys did exactly what I instructed them to do, and when we met the next week, all of them could quote the verse from memory. Not only so, but their entire countenance reflected a willingness and desire to be part of the vitality that was on display here.

Over the next eight to ten years, men's group ministry became an intense school for me. I learned that a men's group really ministers to one another when there are between three to five guys together. As a result, as each group grew, someone would show an aptitude for leadership, and then I, along with another person from that group, would leave to start another one. This became contagious. To see these guys being changed by the strength of the scriptures was a lesson in dynamics. Often, men would be converted to Jesus Christ, and their lives were dramatically changed. Occasionally, I would stop by the workplace of some of the guys just to say hello, and it was easy to find business cards with verses on them in tool boxes, on pickup dashboards, in wallets and checkbooks, inside the rim of their ball caps, and—you name it. They were everywhere. So what happened really isn't that much of a mystery. To begin with, I was selecting verses that seemed to resonate in my spirit. It's not enough to say that we should talk to God in prayer; we should expect that God wants to speak with us personally, and so these verses held that promise. As the Bible says, "so is my word that goes out from my mouth; It will not return to me empty, but will accomplish what I desire and achieve the purpose for which I sent it" (Isaiah 55:11 NIV). Also, the idea of only three to five guys at each meeting told me that when there are more than three people in a conversation, it will begin to divide, not to mention that the confidentiality seems to diminish. So small was good, and it was powerful; lives were changing, and it was contagious. By all rights, this was not supposed to happen. It was a mistake from the onset, except for the fact that over the years, God had built in me an awareness of his very presence in peculiar and often disappointing circumstances. I never asked God to give me power; however, I received it through sensitivity and obedience. This came to be evidence of God's power in human flesh.

Power in Disappointments

In the book of Acts, there is a supernatural energy that is directly related to the Gospels where Jesus was on planet Earth doing his stuff, and his disciples, men and women alike, were affecting their communities, and people by the hundreds were becoming Christ followers. We should desire this in our lives; however, for quite some time, it's become blatantly obvious to me that even many Christians of today just do not believe in the supernatural. It's understandable that we could get caught up with scientific explanations for things, so if there is one, let's accept it. But God is a supernatural God. He was conceived and born supernaturally. He lived and performed miracles and healings that were supernatural. Nowadays, we have modern medicine along with knowledge and science that take us past the stars, but there continue to be so many questions where no one has the answers—only God. The apostle Paul knew that about our Lord, but he had an infirmity, a weakness, and he said it like this: he had a "thorn in his flesh, a messenger of Satan to torment me. Three times I pleaded with the Lord to take it away from me. But he said to me, 'My grace is sufficient for you, my power is made perfect in weakness. Therefore I will boast all the more gladly about my weaknesses, so that Christ's power may rest on me'" (2 Corinthians 12:8–9 NIV, with my own BST version). So Paul's ability to cope was an ongoing appropriation of that strength. Make no mistake. Paul knew about the supernatural. He never questioned God's ability to heal him completely of this physical affliction. However, God had another plan; it was about another dimension of that power! The power that we long to experience in and around our lives comes as the result of resigning our will to God's. We cannot change life's challenging circumstances, and furthermore, we cannot change how God longs to use these to shape us for his purposes. We can only agree with him and ask for his amazing supply.

Paul wasn't alone in the somewhat puzzlement of God's answer to him. There are those who have struggled for much of life, and they have sought God often without an answer, but we can rest assured that God has it all under control. More often than not, this will be a shaping mechanism that will eventually make us do what God needs of us to do his bidding. In the prophet Ezekiel's time, God told him that he was going to give him a hard head—a head, he said, as hard as flint. We can question that all we want; however, God had purposed that he was going to make a man who would stand up to the politics of his time. He said, "I will make you as unyielding and hardened as they are. I will make your forehead like the hardest stone, harder than flint. Do not be afraid of them or terrified by them" (Ezekiel

3:1–16 NIV). God had a message for the people of Ezekiel's time, and to confirm it as well as emphasize the fact, he used flint to demonstrate that hardness. Flint, as you may know, is of sufficient density to strike a light. Again, a display of God's mighty power, only this was the result of accepting a lifetime of difficulty, thereby making Ezekiel somewhat of a callused man. This should make one wonder if in fact our trying times, similar to Ezekiel's, have made in us a person who could be used for the purposes of which only heaven could imagine. It's no mistake that through our trials, not only will we be shaped, but there will be an assignment commensurate with the person we have become.

Power of the Eucharist

In the big picture, I wonder if we as Christians don't frequently look like a ragtag army of misfits. Failure at certain times in our lives has come to define us. As a result, we tend to feel unworthy. We become humbled, yet our tender and thirsting hearts push us forward (forceful like John the Baptist?) In a word, like the natives of long ago, the best of us will become a people of desperation. The prophet Daniel said something that has often come to rescue my damaged feelings, "Some of the wise will stumble, so that they may be refined, purified and made spotless until the end for it will come at an appointed time" (Daniel 11:35 NIV). I have found this to be tremendously comforting, as so often I tend to fall short. We must claim this "refining," however, as it becomes an inner cleansing and consequently a power for the work of the kingdom. We should realize that the need, maybe the pain that we so often experience, is only a reminder, a call if you will, to a greater responsibility. When we feel this way, we must ask God to assist us beyond our natural ability, as this is only a testimonial of sin's encroachment on our community, our nation, and the world. Once we've recognized it as such, it should represent a calling, an invitation to participate on the actual battlefront. In a military sense, we have been made ready to engage. This is our time, our call to duty and our theater of operations.

There is no time that I sense the need for a divine infusion more acutely than during times such as I've written here. Of course we attend services to worship the Lord, to give public reading to the scriptures, and to pray for our community and the world. But the one thing that is so empowering and that my soul so desperately craves is partaking of the Lord's table. This is where we receive from the Lord Jesus the substance, the purifying strength if you will, to be all that we can be for the God we represent. I am frequently honored in our church to serve the Lord's table, either the plate or the cup, and it is humbling to participate in this capacity, the sacrament of the Lord's table. I only wish I could put into words my true feelings as I look into the face of each parishioner and hand them the elements, saying, "The body of Christ" or "The blood of Christ." While we partake together, Jesus is present in his true nature. This isn't just what we say and do; this is what we believe and experience. Consequently, this becomes the literal body and blood of the Lord Jesus. In the Orthodox community of churches, this is called the transubstantiation. While the elements keep their original form, they become the literal body and blood of the Lord Jesus. So let me paint this picture, one where we can contemplate the Lord's table. We can clearly see the priest and his procession as they move from the entrance of the sanctuary, past the baptismal font, and then on to the platform, where he will give the homily. Along with all of the readings of scripture, there will be the prayers by the people for the people, the worship of our tithes and offerings, and then we say the "Our Father." Immediately following, we extend to one another the sign of peace. This all becomes an anticipated performance, one where, regardless of our responsibilities, if we have one or not, we are all invested. This is the assembly! These are the people of God gathered together to celebrate and be empowered. We should recognize this in its entirety. There is power here, in the transubstantiation, the bread and the cup that are no longer just symbolic, the service where the priest and we the people celebrate that there is power for holy living.

Power in Prayer

As we considered the artillery of a Christian warrior, prayer of course is unmistakably our primary weapon. However, until and unless we learn firsthand the power that is available to us here, we are likely to miss the action. There is a tremendous need today for God's people to make prayer a weapon for our time, one where we can see the dirt fly, one where the hierarchy of the devil can be destroyed. We as God's people, no different from the children of Israel, are intended to be instruments of war in the time of God's retribution. In Jeremiah's final prayer, "You are my war club, my weapon for the battle" (Jerimiah 51:20 NIV), these are the murmurs of a man who is watching his community fall to a foreign power, lose their homes, and be taken away because of their sins. Does this sound like something close to our own scenario in America today? Employing the weapon of God, his "war club," requires us individually to be fully submitted to God's will and purposes. This cannot satisfy a heart of vengeance; however, it should be a prayer that is employed when we see corruption within our government and its appointed officials. We must stand against crime. We must stand against those actions that are in violation of the principles of our faith and are biblically corrupt. However, without a genuine love for others, we will fail. In this passage, Jeremiah is recalling the times when God's wrath and retribution waged war against the enemies of his righteousness. This all falls within the God-given ability of each of us, and we will do this day by day as we live for Christ. In this, there is power!

Conclusion

It's important to understand that all of the power spoken of here is of the Holy Spirit. Although it may come by way of a divine anointing following conversion, for sure it will come through obedience. When Jesus was baptized, for example, "heaven was opened and the Holy Spirit descended on him in bodily form like a dove. And a voice came from heaven: 'You are my Son, whom I love, with you I am well pleased'" (Luke 3:21–22 NIV). I find it not only necessary but biblically correct to invite God by his Spirit into my life on a daily basis. The apostle Paul suggests that this be ongoing—that is, to ask for a fresh filling on a regular basis. Here there is power for living. Life and its experiences are a mystery for sure, and we should be glad that we're not all called to be the same and that our performance levels are unique to each of us. What God calls me to do and be and how he wants to affect you will always be vastly different. Are we all expected to be martyrs and give our lives at the stake? Will we each leave a visible mark in our community or nation? I don't think this is what's expected, yet I believe that the Christian community should set the bar a little higher. It's not expected that we attend more church services or join more Christian-based small groups to be what God is asking us to be. But at this time in the history of our world, I believe that God is asking us to get a better focus, one where we can know beyond a doubt that we are getting through to Jesus and that he is getting through to us and to know beyond doubt of the supernatural. This will take a concentrated effort for each of us to become intimately acquainted with our Savior. Although it will take you to places in your Christianity that are past your imagination, so much so that you may question your sanity for asking, it begins with only the whisper of your heart to heaven.

Father God, would you lead me close to your side like no other time in my life? Would you be someone to me whom I have only slightly known previously? I'm not asking for a public voice or a platform but a vibrancy that will be evidence of the reflection of your light shining in and through me. Lord, I want to be sufficiently changed to where your power will affect the circle of my influence and you are forever glorified.

The overall message that's woven tightly into the fabric of this narrative is one of denying self and fully submitting to the Spirit's work in our lives, thereby learning the truth in all situations and applying trust. The stories of God's people throughout the recorded history of the church will testify of this process, and they in turn experienced the power of God. Time is an important factor. Without learning the sensitivity of hearing the Spirit within us, making a mark for eternity will pass us by. Perhaps this is where one should begin. Most of us are people who have an inner desire to be close to Jesus. Somehow, for some, the circumstances of life have told us that we are second rate, not poster-type people, perhaps just average, maybe even a C-. But the Spirit that lies within tells us that we want to belong; we want to be part of an army that is on the move, one where, although operating behind the scenes, we make a difference. We have our own sets of circumstances that oftentimes terrify us, but it's within these circumstances that a passion has somehow been created, a holy drive to rise above and conquer. This is not an element of pride but of a belonging that has significance beyond what positions of pomp have to offer. We are people of purpose, ones who trust in God and believe in the bigger picture. The desires that we have for self and family and business will one day come to pass, but meanwhile, we fervently press toward the mark—the goal of our faith. This is what Jesus asked of his disciples the night of his arrest. This is what was asked of many of the characters of the Old and New Testaments alike, "Would you watch with me one hour?" Jesus is asking that we pray earnestly about our circumstances. It doesn't require intelligence or skill; however, as we engage, prayer fights and frustrates the enemy to win the day. Here there is power.

While traveling at one time in Europe, we viewed a billboard posted in front of a small, stone prison in Rome. The apostle Paul was once supposedly incarcerated there, and it's believed that he wrote many of his letters to the early church from this place. This sign displayed the likeness of Paul; he's old and appears emaciated. He's decrepit and uses a cane. Beneath the picture are some of his own words that were likely written from the dark dampness of his barred captivity: "For me to live is Christ, to die is gain." For some, there will be visible marks of the price they paid to represent the kingdom, and for others, it will be different. What really matters is our dedication to Christ and his agenda for the world.

11

FOR THE BIRDS

I pray also that the eyes of your heart may be enlightened in
order that you may know the hope to which he has called
you, the riches of his glorious inheritance in the saints, and
his incomparably great power for us who believe.
—Ephesians 1:18 (NIV)

As is often the case, we humans could learn some lessons from raw nature
or the unvarnished habits of the animal world. If only a person could
allow their habitually cramped imagination to stretch past the norms of
everyday experience to grasp, if you will, from these lower creatures of habit
a possible thought of enlightenment. For me, most recently, I've seemed to
recapture one of the dynamics of life played out in the arrival of an annual
guest at our home. In the early springtime, we experience the return of
many different birds that have either left our region for the winter or quite
possibly just made themselves less visible. In either case, it's the robins
that tend to be the most obvious summer visitor, and unlike other species
of the winged variety, they don't make their presence known by singing
a song on a nearby fence or the scanty limb of a quaking aspen. They are
just busy finding the right place to build a nest. Nonetheless, springtime
brings them our way again and again, and similar to other years, mother
robin has made her nest at the top of a supporting post in the roof structure
of our backyard deck.

Like most every morning, I rise early to start my day. I'll make a pot
of coffee and find my seat in the family room that overlooks this deck area

mentioned above. In the summertime, it's an inspiring place to be. While we have neighbors on all sides of us, the lawns are quite spacious, and at this early time of day, there are seldom any distractions, such as the noise of a lawn mower or a garden tiller. Fact is, as I write, the only sound that can be heard is that of light rain falling on the rooftops, without even the clap of thunder or the flash of lightning. It's peaceful! Mother bird has not only constructed her nest in the safety of the rafters, but she has obviously laid her eggs and now sits quiet and content, warming her future brood while keeping a watchful eye on her surroundings. This will go on for several weeks until finally we will notice tiny blue eggshells scattered around on the floor, mixed in with the normal construction materials essential for nest building. What a mess this has become, but no one will dare to clean things up; this is just part of what it takes to raise a family of baby robins.

From this point on, a pair of binoculars finds its place on the round table next to my chair, and anyone who happens by may watch for the new babies to show themselves by pointing their hungry little beaks skyward from the nest. And true to form, both mother and dad robin will faithfully shuttle worms from the nearby lawns to the nest. Studies say that the parent robins make as many as one hundred food deliveries a day to sustain the rapid growth of their babies; it is bird and worm arrival—chirp, chirp, chirp, and repeat. This goes on for several weeks until we begin to notice that the babies raise their ugly little heads above the rim of the nest. And then it isn't long until mother and dad will be forced completely out of the nest, and food deliveries, such as they are, will be touch and go. From this point on, the process becomes increasingly educational.

The psyche of the bird world is now on full display. I'm not suggesting that the temperaments that we as humans have will be emulated exactly; however, there are leaders, and there are followers, the timid and the more aggressive. Although you would never see a bird consciously show off to human beings, it does seem that there is the obvious stronger, more dominant bird, and there are those with less determination. And sad as it may be, this determination, or lack of it, becomes the deciding factor for survival in the animal world. I've watched real-life documentaries proving that the offspring of animal populations, when showing twins, triplets, or even quadruplets, are likely to experience one of the batch beginning to fall behind. The parent in these cases will encourage the weaker one only to a point, and if they fail, then they will succumb to nature's cruel fate. No one wants to think about this too seriously because it can become very painful. Not only so, but to go from real-life observation to contemplation, not to mention personal application, is worse still. The punishment seems far too severe, too final. And such is the story of the baby robins.

This year, there are triplets in the nest, three hungry little beaks, three very unattractive little heads, and three growing and ambitious critters of nature, anxiously wanting to leave their nest and strike out for the great unknowns of life. It was the little one in the center toward the back that struggled most intensely in its desperation to have a better perch, one that offered some freedom to stretch its cramped legs and to flutter its wings. This little bird needed space, and with no concern for his siblings, he pushed his way slightly out of the nest to a place on the supporting beam where he was able to exercise. He would go up and down just like someone trying to pull up their trousers, and it was hilariously funny. All in the same spurt of energy, he would extend his wings and flap them around. I question if this was part of a rehearsed strategy for flight; it's what nature designed for him to do. And then, as if to calculate the risk of expressing his true identity, he would look down. This was going to be far more intense than stepping from the nest to the beam; it would be a game changer. Having never used his wings to take him from point A to point B, this would be an exercise of instinctive trust to the max.

It's said that robins tend to take their first flight, for better or for worse, at nighttime. At this point, I have no idea if this is true or not, as I'm just a casual observer. But after watching this seemingly more aggressive bird for an entire day, sometime late in the night, he made his escape. Whatever was to become of him was happening at this very moment. If you were to listen closely outside, you would hear him call out as he hid in the bushes nearby. And one of the parents would faithfully continue to provide food and some measure of protection. This will go on for another two weeks until finally baby robin has learned to more precisely take to the air, not to mention find an adequate supply of food. Then this little bird will become all that he has been intended to be—a cheery songbird, a companion, at one time a parent, and most importantly, a beautiful complement to all of nature.

Meanwhile, back at the nest robin #2 and #3 are still in grave contemplation of the eight- or nine-foot drop from the safety and comfort of their nest to the concrete deck below. Only sensing that they can fly offers little consolation, and all they can do is look down in absolute terror. Eventually, however, the call to be their intended self will rise to the occasion. There is tension here. It's one of life's challenges, and it will taunt them until it has had its way. This is testing the water, so to speak, but it's only a preliminary exercise in leaving the nest. It's not finding food or being protected from a predator or laying their own eggs. It's quite literally just stepping off into what destiny has purposed for them to do; the rest will eventually take care of itself. It was the next night that baby robin #2 followed the call to his or her rightful responsibility. But still the parents would continue to bring an ample supply of worms for robin #3. In suspense over this whole affair, I actually went outside and talked to the bird. "Come on, little buddy, you can do it. Go for it! Don't be left behind. Don't be afraid!"

Now it was the third day since the first of the siblings left the nest, and we felt certain this was going to be the day for the last of the robins to be left at home. It didn't happen. Finally, it was the fourth day, and early in the morning as I went out to encourage this little guy, I could see his mother on the fence close by. She was holding a worm in her beak and waiting patiently for me to leave so she could continue the delivery. Sadly, this would be the last morsel of tender goodness #3 would get, and yet he sat in the nest as if fear had consumed every fiber of his being. The day went slowly, and for me, it was beginning to be painful. Other small birds were darting around under the cover of the deck area, and all too soon, I learned of their intention. Nature was setting its own stage, and I wanted no part of this dastardly affair. I watched until it was late in the evening, and then I spoke with my wife about what was happening. She was intently looking things up on the internet and confirming what I had previously observed outside. I began to do my normal evening chores for bedtime preparation, after which I decided to take one last look into the nest. I didn't like what was happening, and the entire story failed to excite me with any satisfying ending. Quietly, I went to the back door, and with flashlight in hand, I saw that robin #3 was gone. Needless to say, I was ecstatic!

The picture was now complete, I thought; a pair of springtime robins had successfully made a home and raised a small family, sending them out on their own to procreate for themselves. Not surprisingly for me, this memory seems impossible to erase, and those very sensitive observations have tended to live on. Perhaps for each of us, author and reader alike, as we carry on in the mundane exercises of life, there should be an occasional reminder of the robins and the determination they each had for life itself. And while the individuality that typifies our own personality will never be the same, the thought that one cannot deny is that life is a gift, and we each were born for a purpose. If there were no other claim, it might be to pull up our own pants, flap our beautiful wings, and show ourselves off to the world in some glorious way. But wait, that would mean that we've allowed our melancholy personalities freedom to assign a somewhat shallow conclusion to the story, when in actuality, there should be no real ending. Lessons like this are meant to stimulate further brain activity, to go deeper into our very soul where other thoughts of personal conviction may have nudged us more recently. We're not birds! The fact that we do some things instinctively ourselves should never corral the way we think in any way. As humans, we can reason, and we must explore these observations further.

For some, this could defy the way we have looked at life for so long. How are we to be challenged in matters such as the illustration of the robins? I believe that we can begin to ask questions of ourselves. What has been our godly progress as of late? To what disciplines have I been flagging? And so on. This is never easy because, throughout our lives, we have taught ourselves that these are questions for our intellect, and they're not! The intellect wants to rationalize, and we are left to argue with the subject at hand, but we must explore these observations further. This is where the Spirit of our souls longs to surpass the intellect, because it discerns the thoughts and intent of the heart. If allowed, the Spirit will pierce our very soul. Quite often, what goes on in the soul is such a mystery that we aren't even aware of, but like the robins, we are called to something bigger, something more grandiose. But too, like baby robin, we're scared to even look down. For us as humans, to be all that we are intended to be may frequently demand that we combine the instinctive trust of the robins with a tenacious faith in the one who longs to hold us.

This is self-denying; to spiritually fly like the robin, we must abandon the known for the unknown. And finally, as Christians, we must remember that it's only an examined life that is a life worth living. So I will say to you, as I said to the robins and as I say to myself, "Go for it, my friend. You can do it. Don't be left behind! Don't be afraid! What is the Spirit within you saying?" You can recognize him now on the fence top close by, beckoning us each to take flight.

This is not the end. It's only the beginning!

Printed in the United States
by Baker & Taylor Publisher Services